COMMUNITY POLICING THINKERS

COMMUNITY POLICING THINKERS

Lalith Kumar Dharavath

EXCELLER BOOKS®
A GLOBAL PRESS

COMMUNITY POLICING THINKERS

Cover by Exceller Books

Print ISBN: 978-93-47397-56-1

Published in India in 2026 by Exceller Books,
An imprint of GE Group,
G1, Dream Apartment, Degree College Road, Belgharia,
Kolkata, 700056, India
www.excellerbooks.com

EXCELLER BOOKS®
A GLOBAL PRESS

To My Beloved Parents

ACKNOWLEDGEMENT

First of all, I would like to thank God for giving me the strength and patience to complete this book in the limited time available. I would like to thank my parents, wife, children, and friends who helped me complete this book and provided support and encouragement. Once again, I thank all those people who were directly and indirectly involved and supported me in making this book. Thanks again to all those who helped me during the making of the book.

HOW TO USE THIS BOOK

The book is intended for a wide audience, including students of criminal justice, policing scholars, policy experts, and police professionals (ranging from officers to administrators and planners). It is not a "cookbook" with detailed prescriptions for immediate action but rather a resource that provides perspective, context, and guidance for reflective practice. Potential uses include: Students can use it as a primary text to gain an in-depth understanding of the concepts, theory, and research surrounding community policing. Learning objectives, key terms, and discussion questions help structure learning. Law enforcement agencies and training academies can utilize it to train officers and supervisors in community policing principles and problem-solving methods. Scholars and policy experts can draw upon the book's frameworks and case studies to inform discussions and decisions about community safety strategies. Police officers can use the real-life examples in the "Spotlight on Community Policing Practice" sections and problem-solving case studies to apply principles to their daily work, moving from a reactive to a problem-solving orientation.

THE FINAL WORD

The "final word" on Community Policing thinkers is that there is no single consensus; rather, the concept has evolved through the contributions of several key figures and a variety of ongoing research and critiques. The core idea is a shift from police as a "force" to police as a "service," partnering with the public to ensure safety and quality of life.

Sir Robert Peel: Often considered the philosophical father of modern policing, his principles established the idea that "the police are the public and the public are the police," laying the groundwork for police legitimacy built on public trust and consent.

Herman Goldstein: He developed the concept of problem-oriented policing (POP), which shifts the focus from simply responding to individual crimes to identifying and analyzing underlying community problems and developing tailored solutions in partnership with the community. This is a core component of modern community policing strategies.

George L. Kelling: Heco-authored the influential "Broken Windows" theory with James Q. Wilson, which suggested that visible signs of crime and disorder (e.g., broken windows, graffiti) create an environment that encourages more serious crime. This provided a theoretical justification for community policing's focus on order maintenance and quality-of-life issues.

William G. Skogan: He is a prominent researcher who has extensively studied community policing, including its implementation in cities like Chicago. His work highlights the challenges of implementation and the mixed evidence regarding its effectiveness in reducing crime rates, though it consistently shows improvements in citizen satisfaction and police legitimacy. The "final word" remains an active debate due to several factors: there is no single, fixed definition of community policing, making it difficult to consistently measure its effects across programs and jurisdictions. Research offers ambiguous conclusions. While community policing strategies generally improve citizen satisfaction, perceptions of disorder, and police legitimacy, their effect on actual crime and fear of crime is often limited. Critics note that community policing's democratic ideals often conflict with traditional police culture, and effective implementation requires sustained commitment, resources, and genuine community involvement, which are difficult to achieve in practice. Some thinkers argue that the value of community policing lies more in establishing a more just and accountable relationship between police and citizens (procedural justice) than in crime-fighting alone. In essence, the "final word" is an ongoing dialogue: community policing is widely accepted as a vital philosophical foundation for democratic policing, but requires continuous refinement and rigorous, evidence-based implementation to live up to its promises of building trust and enhancing public safety.

PREFACE

The philosophy of community policing has been shaped by a number of key thinkers who advocated a shift from a reactive, solely force-based model of law enforcement to a proactive, collaborative approach involving citizens. Key thinkers and their contributions include **Sir Robert Peel.** Although community policing is a modern term, its core principles trace back to Peel, who established the London Metropolitan Police Force in 1829. His vision was that "the police are the public and the public are the police," emphasizing that police are members of the community whose function is to serve it by consent. In the mid-20th century, as part of the professionalization era, thinkers like Wilson focused on internal management and the "means over ends" approach (efficiency of police organization), which community policing later reacted against. He is a key figure in modern policing thought. In a seminal 1979 article, Goldstein criticized the "means over ends syndrome" in traditional policing and advocated for **Problem-Oriented Policing (POP)**. This approach encouraged police to focus on identifying and solving underlying community problems rather than merely responding to calls and processing cases. Their influential 1982 article (and later book) introduced the **"Broken Windows" theory**. They argued that visible signs of social disorder and neglect (like broken windows) create an environment that encourages more serious crime. This theory provided a strong theoretical justification for proactive police intervention in minor issues in collaboration with the community to prevent urban decay and serious crime. Directors of the National Center for Community Policing at Michigan State University were instrumental in defining and promoting community policing as a philosophy and an organizational strategy. They defined it as a collaboration between the police and the community to identify and solve community problems, with the goal of improving the overall quality of life. Bayley, a scholar who has extensively researched international policing, has analyzed the effectiveness and challenges of community policing. He has explored how enacting community policing policies might impact traditional crime control effectiveness and bureaucratic power. These thinkers provided the philosophical and theoretical foundation for modern community policing, shifting the focus from solely reactive law enforcement to proactive, collaborative, and problem-solving strategies that involve citizens as active partners.

CONTENTS

INTRODUCTION, OUTLINES AND OVERVIEW

Community policing is a philosophy and organizational strategy that emphasizes **police-community partnerships** to address crime, social disorder, and fear of crime. Key thinkers and foundational concepts in its development shifted the paradigm away from a solely reactive law-enforcement model toward one that relies on community input and proactive problem-solving. Community policing is a core strategy for modern law enforcement, aiming to build trust and shared responsibility for public safety. The fundamental belief is that the community is the police's greatest resource and ally in the fight against crime, fostering collaboration among law enforcement agencies, community members, local government, and private organizations. Encouraging police and citizens to work together to identify and address the root causes of specific community problems is a concept often linked to Problem-Oriented Policing (POP), decentralizing police operations and reorienting patrol functions to allow officers to develop a stronger bond with the specific community members and area they serve. The movement gained momentum in the 1980s and 1990s, with several key figures shaping its theory and practice. Their work provided the intellectual foundation and practical guidelines for implementation.

One such prominent figure is **Sir Robert Peel.** Often considered the "father" of modern policing, he established the London Metropolitan Police in 1829, based on the foundational principle that "the police is public, public is police," a core tenet of community policing. He is a major academic influence who developed the concept of **Problem-Oriented Policing (POP)**, arguing that police should focus on specific problems and tailor solutions, rather than just reacting to individual incidents. Their work expanded on POP, notably in "**Who ya gonna call?** The police as problem-busters" (1987), providing early frameworks for problem-solving in a community context. The authors of "Community Policing: A Contemporary Perspective" (1990) provided a comprehensive outline and practical guide that described community policing as a complete shift in policing philosophy. Through works like "Community Policing: Issues and practices around the world" (1988), they provided a global perspective on different approaches and the challenges of implementing community policing. These thinkers and their related works outlined the shift from a professional, often distant, police model to one that requires collaboration, trust, and shared responsibility with the communities they serve.

Introduction Outlines

Community policing thinkers write books to advocate for a fundamental shift from traditional, reactive policing to a proactive, collaborative approach that involves citizens in solving community problems. These authors seek to define the philosophy, share implementation strategies, evaluate effectiveness, and guide future practices for law enforcement and communities worldwide. Community policing thinkers write these books because the field lacks a single, universal definition; they aim to clarify its core concepts, which typically include citizen involvement, problem-solving, and the decentralization of authority. Many books emerge from the recognition that the traditional, incident-driven police model is insufficient for addressing complex issues like fear of crime, social disorder, and neighborhood decay. The authors aim to offer practical advice, strategies, and "roadmaps" to help police administrators and street-level officers successfully transition from traditional methods to community policing. A primary goal is to improve public confidence in the police and enhance police legitimacy by fostering mutual respect, understanding, and cooperation between law enforcement and the communities they serve. Thinkers in the field publish empirical studies and evaluations of community policing initiatives to separate "fact from fiction," highlight successes and failures, and inform evidence-based practices. Books are often written to influence policymakers, academicians, and the public, promoting community policing as the most appropriate philosophical foundation for modern, democratic policing. Comparative analyses of community policing in different countries help show how the approach is interpreted and implemented across diverse cultural and political contexts, addressing global challenges. These books serve as a bridge between the theory and everyday practice of police reform, aiming to enhance public safety and the quality of life in communities.

Traditional Policing Model

The evolution of the police role has shifted significantly from a traditional, reactive, "enforce and control" model to a proactive, collaborative approach known as community policing. The traditional model, prevalent for much of the 19th and 20th centuries, was characterized by police responding primarily after incidents occurred. The police force was often a top-down, hierarchical bureaucracy with limited discretion given to lower-ranking officers on the beat. The focus was on individual crimes and arrests, not the underlying causes of crime or disorder. Officers had minimal interaction with community members beyond formal enforcement actions, leading to a sense of detachment and potential mistrust. The widespread use of police cars reduced officer interaction and familiarity with the specific geographic areas they patrolled.

The Evolution to Community Policing

The shift towards community policing was a response to the limitations of the traditional model and civil unrest in the mid-to-late 20th century. This evolution introduced several key changes. This approach emphasizes understanding and addressing the root causes of crime and disorder rather than focusing solely on immediate incidents. Law enforcement agencies actively listen to community concerns and form partnerships with citizens, local businesses, non-profits, and other government entities to collaboratively develop solutions. The focus moved from mere response to active crime prevention through collaboration and community involvement, such as neighborhood watch groups and youth clubs. There has been a move toward some decentralization of police authority, allowing officers more discretion and initiative on their beats, coupled with increased accountability to the communities they serve. The reintroduction of specific geographic assignments, often with officers on foot or bicycle patrols, allowed officers to build familiarity and trust within the neighborhood's social fabric. The modern approach often involves collaborating with social services, mental health resources, and youth programs to address socioeconomic problems that contribute to crime, which are often beyond the sole scope of law enforcement. In essence, the role has expanded from merely "enforcing the law" to "producing safety and security" in cooperation with the public, grounded in the principle that "the police are the public and the public are the police".

The Crisis in Traditional Policing Defines

The "crisis" in traditional policing is defined by a confluence of systemic issues, most notably a lack of public trust and confidence, the perceived ineffectiveness of traditional reactive strategies, and persistent problems of police misconduct and a lack of accountability. The crisis of traditional police administration stems from its reactive, incident-driven approach, which has led to a breakdown of public trust, political interference, and organizational inefficiencies. These limitations prevent it from effectively addressing the complex underlying causes of modern crime and social issues. Traditional police administration is often viewed by thinkers and academicians as a bureaucratic, law-enforcement-focused model with an emphasis on hierarchy, control, and a "crime-control" mission. Key critiques highlight its roots in an authoritarian past and its disconnect from community needs in modern democratic societies. The crisis in traditional policing has been a central topic for various thinkers, particularly in the fields of criminology, sociology, and public policy. Key figures and their central arguments include:

Herman Goldstein: Often described as a leading figure in the critique of traditional, reactive policing, Herman Goldstein argued that the field had become overly focused on the "means" of policing (e.g., response times, arrests) rather than the "ends" or goals of reducing crime and disorder. He introduced problem-oriented policing (POP) as a paradigm shift, advocating a proactive approach in which police identify and analyze the underlying causes of recurring community problems and work with other agencies to develop tailored, non-law-enforcement solutions. Critical Criminologists (e.g., Tony Platt, Paul Chevigny, Stuart Hall) During the 1970s, Marxist and critical Anglo-American criminologists analyzed the role of police within broader societal power structures. Paul Chevigny (1969) argued that the criminal justice system is "evil" because it injures people and destroys their respect for the legal process, with police abuses serving as symbols of oppression, particularly in marginalized communities. Stuart Hall and his co-authors of the influential book *Policing the Crisis* examined police-state-class relationships, focusing on how law enforcement practices were tied to social and political crises in advanced capitalist societies.

James Q. Wilson: In his classic studies of police work, James Q. Wilson highlighted the inherent difficulties in policing due to a lack of consensus on appropriate police behavior. He noted that this ambiguity makes it hard for officers to do their job properly and easy for them to be penalized for doing it "improperly" in the opinion of others. He also co-authored the influential (and later critiqued) "Broken Windows" theory with George Kelling, which emphasized the importance of addressing minor disorder to prevent serious crime.

Contemporary Thinkers & Movements: More recently, thinkers have emerged within the context of the "defund the police" and Black Lives Matter movements, which gained prominence after the murder of George Floyd in 2020. These contemporary perspectives include activists and thinkers advocating for reallocating police funds to community services, mental health support, and other programs to address the root causes of crime and social problems, thereby preventing people from entering the criminal justice system in the first place. Researchers like Luke William Hunt are exploring the "police identity crisis," examining how police forces navigate conflicting roles as "hero, warrior, guardian, [and] algorithm" in modern society. Scholars on procedural justice argue that past reforms have failed because they do not adequately measure how people are treated by the police, proposing new accountability systems using data from body-worn cameras and contact surveys to build police legitimacy. These thinkers provide diverse frameworks for understanding the current challenges facing traditional policing models and propose radical departures from established practices. Addressing the crisis in traditional policing requires a multifaceted approach that increases accountability and transparency, implements community-oriented policing models, improves training and resources, and leverages technology and specialized responses.

Independent Oversight: Establish independent civilian oversight bodies and police complaints authorities to investigate misconduct, which can help ensure impartial reviews and increase public confidence.

Mandatory Data Collection and Reporting: Implement systems for rigorous record-keeping and the collection of disaggregated data (e.g., on use of force, stop-and-search incidents, and complaints) to identify potential biases and problematic practices.

Use of Technology for Evidence: Mandate the use of body-worn cameras to provide an objective record of interactions between officers and the public, promoting responsible behavior from both sides.

Public Access to Information: Ensure transparency by making police policies, data on citizen complaints, and outcomes of investigations publicly accessible to foster informed citizen engagement, shift from an "us vs. them" mentality to a collaborative problem-solving approach where police work with community members, local organizations, and social agencies to address the root causes of crime and disorder.

Beat Policing Systems: Revive or strengthen systems where officers are assigned to specific geographic areas long-term to build relationships, gather local intelligence, and address community-specific needs. Emphasize treating all citizens with fairness, dignity, and respect to build trust and legitimacy, which is a fundamental principle for effective policing. Provide extensive, ongoing training in de-escalation techniques, mental health crisis management, active listening, and cultural competency to equip officers with the skills needed for diverse situations. Develop tiered response models where civilians or specialized professionals (e.g., social workers, mental health experts) are the primary responders for non-violent crises like mental health calls or homelessness, freeing up police resources and ensuring appropriate expertise is applied. Tackle understaffing through improved recruitment strategies, better working conditions, competitive pay, and mental health support to attract and retain qualified personnel. Implement reforms to ensure police autonomy by creating independent boards for personnel decisions (transfers, promotions) and establishing State Security Commissions to insulate forces from undue political pressure. Utilize data analysis, academic research, and the testing of different tactics to determine the most effective strategies for crime control and resource allocation. Leverage technology for enhanced efficiency and crime prevention, including AI for data analysis, online reporting apps, and modern communication tools, while also addressing privacy and ethical concerns. Create specialized units or cadres, such as those focused on cybercrime or financial fraud, to address the evolving nature of modern offences. Traditional policing, often defined by its reactive "call-to-call" approach, has demonstrably failed to adequately address community safety in a comprehensive manner [1]. This model prioritizes responding to incidents after they have already occurred, rather than proactively preventing them, leading to a number of critical shortcomings.

Shortcomings of the Traditional Policing Model

The reliance on emergency response means that root causes of crime are rarely addressed [1]. This constant reaction creates a cycle where police are always playing catch-up, rather than working to stop crime before it happens. Traditional policing practices can foster a disconnect between law enforcement and the public, often relying on a focus on brute force and enforcement tactics that can damage public perception [1]. This creates significant barriers to effective law enforcement, as residents may be hesitant to report crimes, provide witness testimony, or cooperate with investigations. The "us versus them" mentality inherent in some traditional models leads to a significant breakdown in communication and partnership between the police and the community [1]. Without community buy-in, law enforcement efforts are often less effective, as officers lack the local intelligence and support needed for effective problem-solving.

Community Policing as a Modern Solution

To address these failures, community policing has emerged as a proactive, collaborative, and modern approach [1]. This strategy requires a fundamental shift in philosophy, moving away from the reactive model to one that fosters partnerships and shared responsibility [1]. Key elements of the community policing approach include:

Instead of waiting for a call to emergency services, community policing involves officers engaging with residents through strategies like foot patrols and community meetings [1]. This consistent presence helps officers better understand local concerns and build relationships. Police work hand in hand with residents, local businesses, and community organizations to identify and solve the underlying problems that contribute to crime [1]. This collaborative problem-solving approach empowers the community and gives residents a voice in their own safety. By prioritizing communication, transparency, and collaboration, community policing aims to rebuild and foster trust between the police and the community [1]. The goal of this shift is to create a true partnership where both police and community members work together to solve problems and prevent crime [1]. This is intended to lead to enhanced public safety, stronger police-community relations, and a greater level of public trust in law enforcement agencies.

Traditional policing is primarily reactive, focusing on responding to crimes after they occur, whereas community-oriented policing is proactive, aiming to prevent crime by addressing root causes and fostering positive relationships within the community.

Incident-driven: Police primarily respond to calls for service, meaning they address crimes after they have happened.

Visible Presence: Maintaining a visible presence through patrolling is a key aspect of traditional policing. Traditional policing often emphasizes apprehending suspects and clearing cases, which can lead to higher arrest rates.

Hierarchical Structure: Traditional policing typically has a more hierarchical organizational structure with clear lines of authority.

Limited Community Engagement: Traditional policing may have less emphasis on actively engaging with the community to understand and address their concerns.

Example Scenario: If a fight breaks out in a park, a traditional policing approach would primarily involve dispatching officers to the scene to arrest the individuals involved. They might then investigate the incident after the fact. However, they may not delve into the underlying reasons for the fight or implement preventive measures to stop similar incidents from happening again.

ContrastwithCommunity-OrientedPolicing

Community-oriented policing (COP) takes a more holistic approach by focusing on problem-solving, collaboration with the community, and preventing crime from occurring in the first place.

Proactive Approach

COP actively identifies and addresses the root causes of crime by working with community members to develop solutions.

Community Engagement

COP emphasizes building relationships and trust with the community through initiatives such as community meetings and foot patrols.

Partnership with Stakeholders

COP involves various stakeholders, such as schools, businesses, and social service organizations, in addressing community problems.

Focus on Long-term Solutions

COP aims to create sustainable changes in the community by addressing the underlying issues that contribute to crime. Using the same scenario of a fight in the park, a COP approach would involve investigating the causes of the conflict, perhaps by engaging with residents, local businesses, and youth organizations to understand the underlying issues. They might implement programs or initiatives to address these issues, such as conflict-resolution workshops or expanded recreational opportunities. They would also work to build relationships with the community to prevent future incidents.

For a more helpful explanation of multiple-choice questions, try including the answer options in your search.

Key Differences
Traditional policing, also known as reactive policing, focuses on responding to crimes after they occur, whereas proactive policing aims to prevent crime by actively engaging with the community and identifying potential criminal activity before it escalates.

Response to Crime

Reactive Policing
Officers primarily respond to calls for service, arriving at crime scenes after the incident has taken place.

Proactive Policing
Officers actively patrol areas with high crime rates, engage with community members to gather information on potential issues, and implement strategies to deter crime before it occurs.

Reactive Policing
Primarily focuses on apprehending suspects and solving crimes after they occur. Emphasizes crime prevention through visible presence, community engagement, and addressing the underlying causes of crime.

Reactive Policing
Routine patrols, investigations following reports of crime, and responding to calls for service.

Proactive Policing
Increased visibility in high-crime areas, community policing initiatives, targeted enforcement of specific crimes, and problem-solving approaches.

Reactive Policing: An officer responding to a robbery in progress.

Proactive Policing

- Conducting foot patrols in a known drug trafficking area,
- Implementing a community policing program to address neighborhood concerns, or establishing a crime prevention hotline.

The user provided a detailed passage discussing the place-based approach to crime reduction, focusing specifically on hotspot policing strategies. This content explains how concentrating police resources in high-crime areas can effectively deter crime and maximize police efforts. The passage notes that police departments can use a range of proactive policing interventions, including problem-oriented policing and direct patrol. Other related strategies mentioned include closed-circuit television (CCTV) monitoring. The core idea of this approach, developed by Sherman and Weisburd in 1995, is that crime is not randomly distributed but highly concentrated in small "hot spots." Focusing resources on these specific areas has been shown to significantly reduce crime and disorder.

Characteristics of Traditional Policing

Traditional policing is a reactive, incident-driven model where police respond to calls for service, focus on apprehending criminals, and are judged by their efficiency in doing so. In contrast to proactive community policing, which seeks to address the root causes of crime, traditional policing's reactive nature means it addresses symptoms, such as arresting youth during a crime surge, rather than underlying issues. This approach can yield short-term results and potentially foster public distrust, as it relies on one-way communication and may not improve overall public safety. Police are primarily mobilized by public calls for service, leading them to respond to incidents after they occur.

The focus is on handling specific incidents as they happen, rather than on preventing them before they occur.

A key objective is to apprehend criminals and deter crime through a strong, visible presence, with professional performance often measured by arrest rates. It fosters a model where police are seen as a distinct segment of the criminal justice system, and community members are expected to support police, rather than partnering with them. This model often employs a hierarchical leadership style in which authority is derived from specific roles and responsibilities, which can lead to negative public perceptions.

Characteristics of Community Policing

Community policing is a proactive strategy that builds relationships with the public to identify and solve problems, aiming to prevent crime and create a safer environment. Traditional policing is a reactive strategy in which police respond to incidents after they occur, through patrols and quick responses to calls for service. Community policing is generally more effective at crime prevention because it fosters collaboration and addresses the root causes of crime through partnerships between the police and the community, ultimately leading to fewer calls for service. Traditional policing is proactive, collaborative, and problem-oriented. It prevents crime by working with the community to identify and address problems that drive criminal activity.

Approach

- Building strong relationships with community members.
- Identifying the root causes of crime and disorder.
- Working together with the community to implement solutions.

Outcomes

- Increased public participation in safety initiatives.
- A greater sense of community and public safety.
- Fewer calls for police service due to proactive problem-solving.

The Goal of Traditional Policing

- To enforce laws and maintain order by responding to crimes after they have happened.
- Officers remain detached from the community.
- Focus on routine patrols to deter crime through visible presence.
- Respond quickly to calls for service.
- Effective for responding to immediate crises.
- Can lead to a cycle of reaction rather than prevention.

Contrast with Community Policing

Community policing seeks to build partnerships between the police and the community to proactively solve problems by identifying and addressing the underlying causes of crime. In response to increased youth violence, community policing would investigate causes and support programs to prevent violence, while traditional policing would focus on short-term solutions.

Comparative Overview: Community Policing and Traditional Policing

Community policing is a proactive, partnership-based approach that involves citizens in preventing crime and improving the quality of life, while traditional policing is a reactive, enforcement-focused model centered on responding to incidents and measuring success by arrests and crime rates. Community policing fosters trust and cooperation through continuous neighborhood presence and citizen engagement, whereas traditional policing often results in one-way communication and limited public partnership. Community policing is proactive and preventive, focusing on building partnerships with the community to address the root causes of crime. In community policing, the police are active partners in crime prevention, with their priorities shaping law enforcement efforts. They are visible, approachable, and continuously engaged in a specific area to build relationships and trust. Success is measured by the quality of life in the community, increased public trust, and reduced crime rates. Collaboration between the police and citizens is essential for creating safer communities. Community policing is characterized by partnerships between the police and the community, problem-solving to address the root causes of crime, and a focus on prevention rather than just reaction. Key characteristics of community policing also include decentralizing authority for local officers, increasing officer accountability, and using more community-oriented training, such as communication skills and cultural competency.

Core Characteristics

A collaborative relationship is built among the police, community members, local government, and other organizations to address public safety and community needs. This approach identifies the underlying causes of crime and disorder, using techniques such as the SARA model (Scanning, Analysis, Response, and Assessment) to identify and implement solutions. The emphasis is on proactively preventing crime through community engagement and addressing social issues, rather than simply reacting to incidents after they happen. More decision-making authority is given to lower-ranked officers, enabling them to exercise greater discretion and initiative in responding to local needs. There is a greater emphasis on accountability to the community the police serve, which is often achieved through long-term assignments and transparent evaluation of performance.

Police officers receive training to improve communication skills, conflict resolution, and cultural competency, to better serve diverse communities and foster trust. Examples of community-focused activities include foot and bicycle patrols to increase visibility and interaction, neighborhood watch programs, community meetings and forums, collaborating with social services to connect people with resources such as mental health support and youth programs, and informal activities like "Coffee with a Cop" to build relationships in a non-enforcement context.

Community Policing Theories

Community policing is supported by theories of participatory governance and social capital, which emphasize collaboration between police and citizens. Key theories include the Broken Windows Theory, which suggests that addressing minor disorder can prevent serious crime, and Social Disorganization Theory, which posits that police-community partnerships can restore social order in communities with weak social institutions. Another important theoretical foundation is Normative Sponsorship Theory, which assumes people are good and willing to cooperate with police to solve problems. These theories are the foundation of community policing, emphasizing that a healthy society requires collaborative problem-solving and cooperation between law enforcement and the community.

Broken Windows Theory

This theory posits that visible signs of crime, anti-social behavior, and civil disorder—such as broken windows—create an environment that encourages more serious crime. Therefore, addressing minor signs of disorder can prevent more significant problems from developing.

Social Disorganization Theory

This theory suggests that crime is more likely to occur in communities with weak social institutions. Community policing, by strengthening these institutions and building social ties, can help to reduce crime.

Normative Sponsorship Theory

This theory assumes that most people are of good will and are willing to cooperate with others to meet their needs. In this context, community policing fosters cooperation between citizens and police to solve problems and improve the community's quality of life.

Critical Social Theory

This theory helps police and citizens understand the root causes of their problems and work together to solve them more effectively. Police officers act as facilitators, guiding the problem-solving process alongside community members.

Drawbacks of Community Policing

Drawbacks of community policing include the need for genuine community trust and involvement, which can be difficult to build and maintain, leading to potential failure if trust is not established. Other disadvantages include a lack of resources and funding, difficulty in defining and including a diverse "community," institutional resistance within the police force, potential favoritism toward certain community groups, and the risk that programs will be used for political gain or personal agendas rather than for community improvement.

Challenges in Implementation

Lackof Trust and Involvement

Community policing fails if there is not a strong, trusting partnership between the police and the community. A lack of trust, fear, or a lack of time commitment from residents can hinder participation.

"The Community"

It can be challenging to determine who represents the "community" and ensure broad, equitable participation from all residents, not just homeowners or specific groups.

Insufficient Resources and Funding

Running community policing programs can be expensive, requiring more officers and overtime, and many departments struggle with budget constraints.

Institutional Resistance

Existing police departments may resist a shift away from traditional policing, and some officers may not embrace the community-oriented philosophy.

Potential for Corruption or Bias

Close ties to the community can be misused for political ends or personal gain, or lead to favoritism toward more privileged groups, ignoring the needs of less privileged residents.

Lackof Strategic Planning

Without proper strategic planning, community policing can become a superficial "shell" that does not address core strategic issues, or it can be implemented without sufficient evaluation or lesson learning.

Potential for Negative Perceptions

Increased Intrusiveness

The close involvement can lead to police becoming overly intrusive into residents' private lives.

Resentment and Distrust

If poorly implemented, community policing can be perceived as aggressive, creating resentment and further eroding trust instead of building it.

Traditional Policing

Traditional policing is reactive, responding to calls for service after a crime has occurred. It is primarily seen as those who report crime, with limited involvement in law enforcement strategy. The main purpose of traditional policing is to enforce laws, maintain order, and respond to criminal activity. Its success is primarily measured by arrest rates and response times. Law enforcement operates with a hierarchical, role-based structure focused on professional duties and authority. Traditional policing is characterized by a reactive, incident-driven approach focused on responding to calls, investigating crimes after they occur, and maintaining a visible presence through random patrol. This model prioritizes law enforcement and employs a hierarchical, authoritative leadership style, often with a "crime-fighting" mentality and a lesser emphasis on community engagement and crime prevention.

Foundational Thinkers

The primary historical thinkers who developed the concepts that underpin traditional policing (the reactive, incident-driven, and centralized model that dominated the mid-20th century) are Sir Robert Peel, August Vollmer, and O.W. Wilson.

Sir Robert Peel (1788-1850)

Often considered the "father of modern policing", Peel, as the British Home Secretary, established the London Metropolitan Police in 1829. The principles attributed to him (the Peelian Principles) provided the philosophical blueprint for early traditional policing. These include: The primary goal is the prevention of crime. Police must secure the public's respect and cooperation to be effective ("policing by consent"). Police should be organized along military lines with a centralized command. Officers should be uniformed, paid, and professional. Physical force should be used only as a last resort.

August Vollmer (1876-1955)

As the police chief in Berkeley, California (1905-1932), Vollmer was a leading figure in the American "police professionalism" movement and is often called the "father of modern law enforcement" in the United States. He advocated for a more efficient and less politically corrupt police force. His contributions to the traditional model include: Implementing psychological and intelligence testing for recruits; utilizing scientific methods in criminal investigations, including forensic laboratories; establishing the first formal police training academies; and promoting the idea of police officers as a professional civil service, distinct from local politics.

Wilson (1900-1972)

A student of Vollmer, Wilson championed the use of technology and scientific management to increase police efficiency. He advocated for: Motorized patrols and two-way radios to enable rapid response to calls for service; rotating officers between different community beats to discourage corruption and build a more impartial force; and focusing on serious felonies and other major crimes rather than less serious "order maintenance" issues.

These thinkers helped shape the traditional, centralized, and reactive policing model that dominated much of the 20th century, which focused on a professional, swift response to reported incidents rather than proactive community engagement.

Core Components

Traditional policing is a reactive, law-enforcement-focused model characterized by responding to calls, investigating crimes after they happen, and maintaining a visible presence through patrol and a focus on arrests and investigations. It originated in a professionalization movement that separated police from the communities they served, prioritizing a crime-fighting approach over community engagement.

Reactive Response

Police actions are primarily initiated by public calls for service.

Law Enforcement Focus: The primary mission is to investigate and apprehend criminals and deter crime through a strong, visible presence.

Crime-fighting Model

It emphasizes outcomes such as arrest numbers and response times.

Separation from the Community
A key aspect of the professionalization era was the detachment of police from the public, leading to a "one-way communication" dynamic.

Organizational Structure
It is often defined by a clear hierarchy and defined roles.
Visible Patrol: Routine patrolling is used to maintain a visible presence and deter crime.
Investigation: A significant portion of police work is dedicated to investigating crimes after they have occurred.

Criticisms of Limited Community Engagement
The model can lead to a lack of cooperation and trust between the police and the community.

Reactive Nature: It is not proactive in preventing crime before it happens, as it relies on calls for service to initiate action. Police primarily react to crimes and calls for service rather than focusing on prevention. The main goal is to enforce laws and combat crime, with less emphasis on crime prevention or community service. A visible police presence is maintained through random, routine patrols. A key performance indicator is the speed at which officers respond to calls. Investigative work is a central component, conducted after a crime has already taken place. Leadership is often described as strict, rules-based, and military-like, with less room for officer discretion or community input. There is often a lack of cooperation and one-way communication between the police and residents. This culture prioritizes an aggressive, confrontational style of policing. Traditional policing is based on the reactionary model of law enforcement, which focuses on responding to crimes after they occur and is often characterized by patrolling and apprehending criminals. Key theories underpinning this approach include the idea that the primary role of police is to investigate crimes and apprehend offenders, with the community's role being limited to supporting the police. Theoretical frameworks such as functionalism and organizational theory have been used to explain the limitations of this model, including its reactive nature and limited public cooperation.

Reactive and Incident-Based
Police are primarily mobilized in response to public calls, making the system reactive rather than proactive.

Focus on Enforcement: Professionalism is often measured by outcomes like arrests and successful responses to calls.

Deterrence Theory
Traditional policing operates on the belief that its presence and enforcement activities will deter criminal activity.

Hierarchical and Top-down
Authority is derived from strict adherence to roles and responsibilities, with a traditional leadership style where officers often take orders from higher authorities.

Theoretical Frameworks

Functionalism
The theory views the police as one part of the larger criminal justice system, with the principal mission of investigating and apprehending criminals.

Organizational Theory
The theory analyzes the structure and function of police organizations to understand their limitations, particularly within the traditional model.

Classical Theory (In Criminology)

While not a policing theory itself, it is an influential background theory that emphasizes free will and rationality on the part of the criminal actor, which informs the focus on individual deterrence and punishment within traditional policing.

Limitations of Traditional Policing

The model fosters a disconnect between police and the community through one-way communication and a lack of public involvement in problem-solving. By focusing solely on incident response, traditional policing is often ineffective at addressing the root causes of crime. Many traditional theories and methods are proving inadequate in new and evolving crime environments, such as cybercrime, due to the lack of visibility and direct community interaction.

Drawbacks of Traditional Policing

Traditional policing has several drawbacks, including a focus on symptoms rather than causes, a reactive rather than proactive approach, a lack of community trust, and potential for ineffectiveness. Key drawbacks include officer isolation from the public, reliance on often-ineffective random patrols, and a tendency to be reactive to incidents rather than preventing them.

Reactive Instead of Proactive

Traditional policing primarily reacts to crime after it occurs, rather than taking proactive steps to prevent it in the first place.

Ignores Root Causes

This model focuses on crime-related symptoms (e.g., arrests) but fails to address underlying issues such as poverty, unemployment, and social disorganization, which are more effective long-term solutions.

Officer Isolation

The professional model can lead officers to spend most of their time with other officers rather than with the public, creating a disconnect and fostering a sense of isolation from the community they serve.

Limited Community Relations

This approach can result in a one-way communication model, with limited cooperation and partnership between police and community members, thereby negatively impacting public trust.

Ineffective Patrol Strategies

Research shows that random preventive patrol is often no more effective than other strategies, and focusing on low-crime areas can be a costly waste of resources.

Lackof Community Buy-In

The public may perceive the police as an external, enforcement-focused force, which can undermine community cooperation and trust, especially if they feel they are not being heard.

Limited Effectiveness

The focus on apprehension and response, rather than prevention, can make the model less effective at achieving long-term crime control than community-oriented models.

Comparative Overview

Feature	Community Policing	Traditional Policing
Focus	Proactive crime prevention	Reactive crime response
Relationship with Community	Partnership and collaboration	One-way communication and enforcement
Key Strategy	Building trust and long-term relationships	Responding to calls and making arrests
Success Metrics	Quality of life, public trust, crime reduction	Crime rates, arrest numbers

Table 1.1

Foundational Thinkers and Concepts

Key thinkers and developers of community policing theory and philosophy include Sir Robert Peel, Herman Goldstein, James Q. Wilson, George L. Kelling, and Robert Trojanowicz.

Sir Robert Peel

Considered the father of modern policing, Peel established the London Metropolitan Police Force in 1829 based on principles that form the historical foundation of community policing. His principles emphasize that the police are the public and the public are the police, and that police should seek to prevent crime and earn public trust and cooperation, rather than rely on force.

Herman Goldstein

A key figure in developing the concept of Problem-Oriented Policing (POP), Goldstein argued that the police should move beyond simply reacting to incidents and instead proactively identify and address the underlying causes of recurring community problems. POP is a core component of modern community policing strategies.

James Q. Wilson and George L. Kelling

Their influential 1982 article "Broken Windows" proposed the "Broken Windows" theory, which posits that visible signs of neighborhood disorder (such as unrepaired windows) invite further social disorder and serious criminal activity. They argued that police, in partnership with the community, should focus on maintaining order to prevent more serious crime, a concept central to community policing's focus on quality-of-life issues.

Robert Trojanowicz and Bonnie Bucqueroux

These scholars provided practical frameworks for implementing community policing. They defined it as a "new philosophy of policing" in which officers and citizens work together to solve community problems related to crime, fear of crime, and neighborhood decay. Trojanowicz also founded the National Center for Community Policing at Michigan State University.

Other Notable Contributors

John Alderson

He approached community policing from a conceptual standpoint, emphasizing policing "under conditions of freedom" and the guarantee of personal liberties.

David H. Bayley and Jerome H. Skolnick

They conducted extensive research and published influential works analyzing the variations and realities of community policing implementation worldwide.

Kenneth Peak

He described the evolution of community policing in the United States through distinct generations: innovation, diffusion, and institutionalization.

Gary Cordner

He is a prominent scholar who has written on the core elements and effects of community policing.

These thinkers moved the philosophy of policing from a reactive, reform-era model focused solely on law enforcement to a proactive, community-centered approach that values public trust, collaboration, and problem-solving.

Principles and Goals

Community policing is a philosophy and strategy where law enforcement builds partnerships with the community to prevent crime and ensure public safety. This approach involves police working closely with citizens to address the root causes of crime and disorder, fostering mutual trust and cooperation to improve the quality of life in a neighborhood. The core idea is to integrate police into the community so that a "policeman is a citizen with a uniform, and a citizen is a policeman without one".

Partnership

It emphasizes a collaborative relationship between the police and the community, in which both parties work together to solve problems.

Proactive Approach

It moves beyond reacting to crime to proactively addressing its causes and preventing it from happening in the first place.

Decentralization

Officers are often assigned to specific neighborhoods for extended periods to build familiarity and stronger relationships with residents.

Improved Trust

By increasing interaction and cooperation, community policing aims to reduce the "trust deficit" between the police and the public.

Problem-solving

Police work with community members to identify and resolve local conflicts and other issues affecting public safety and quality of life.

Citizen Participation

The community takes an active role in identifying local issues, with the police acting as facilitators to help address them.

Police Role: Officers are expected to become an integrated part of the community they serve, rather than remaining distant figures.

Organizational Change

It often requires police departments to change their management style and personnel structures to support partnerships and problem-solving initiatives.

Examples: Projects like the Janamaithri SurakshaProject in Kerala and Joint Patrolling Committees in Rajasthan are examples of community policing initiatives.

Conclusion

Many police departments adopt proactive policing strategies to reduce and control crime. While some proactive policing strategies have failed to generate a positive impact on crime reduction, many others proved to be effective. Each police department should examine its community's problems and needs to choose the best strategies to fight crime. Police departments need to strengthen their relationships with their communities to secure their "buy-in" and cooperation in crime prevention efforts. The police departments will need to hear from the community, listen to their concerns and problems, and collectively work to resolve them. Before selecting any proactive policing approach, a police department should do its best to analyze and understand the problems in the community, then identify the most suitable tactics to resolve these problems. It is very important that the police department monitor and review the impact of the selected policing approach and make adjustments when needed to improve its efforts to prevent crime.

Book: An Overview

The book you are referring to is likely an introductory textbook on policing, such as *Community Policing: A Contemporary Perspective* by Victor E. Kappeler, Larry K. Gaines, and Brian P. Schaefer, or a similar work. The evolution of policing generally traces three major eras: the Political Era, the Reform Era (or Professional Era), and the Community Era.

Early Models (e.g., London Metropolitan System): Modern policing has roots in earlier, often informal, systems of maintaining order. A pivotal development was the establishment of the London Metropolitan Police in 1829 by Sir Robert Peel. This model introduced principles such as policing by consent, a structured organization, and a focus on crime prevention, which influenced policing globally, including in the United States.

In the US, the Political Era (roughly mid-19th century to early 20th century) was characterized by police controlled by local politicians and often mired in corruption. This led to the Reform Era (roughly 1920s to 1970s), which emphasized professionalism, centralization of command, and a focus on crime-fighting through motorized patrol and rapid response to calls. This period aimed to distance police from political influence and establish them as efficient, objective law enforcement professionals.

The social unrest and civil rights movement of the 1960s and 1970s exposed significant rifts between the police and the communities they served, particularly minority groups. High crime rates and a lack of public trust highlighted the limitations of the isolated, traditional crime-fighting model. This period saw a rise in calls for police accountability and better community relations.

These challenges prompted a move toward the Community Policing Era (starting in the 1980s). This philosophy broadens the police mandate to include solving community problems and forming partnerships with the citizenry to proactively address the underlying conditions that give rise to crime and social disorder. It emphasizes foot patrols, community engagement, and mutual responsibility for public safety, aiming to rebuild trust and legitimacy.

Influences on Policing from England, as well as the Impacts of Sir Robert Peel and Chief August Vollmer

We will also review the disturbing histories of how some have been discriminated against and even targeted by police based on their race. As these historical events and influences are discussed, reflect on how they have impacted certain groups and communities more negatively than others. The terms "police officer" and "law enforcement officer" are used interchangeably without any gender reference, but what should be noted is the phrasing difference between "policeman/men" and "police officer." This differentiation was intentional on the authors' part, as throughout many of the policing eras, women were generally not allowed to work in the profession. If they were hired, it was under a microscopic view of certain stereotypical "matronly" duties. Some of these will be discussed in further detail within the section. The other noteworthy point is the reference to "policeman/men" being predominantly White, as men of color, and more specifically, Black men, were rarely hired. A few Black policemen made their way into policing in the late 1800s in the northern states. Still, when the Civil Rights Act of 1875 was ruled unconstitutional, most Black police officers disappeared from policing until the 1950s. This will be explained further within the section.

The development of policing in the United States coincided with the development of policing in England. The United States' legal system traces its roots back to the common law of England. However, looking back before 1750 BC to see how forms of policing were common during ancient times is now known as kin policing. Kin policing is when a tribe or clan policed their own tribe, and it often turned bloody quickly. The blood feuds would last for long periods (Berg, 1999). However, it is estimated that the Code of Hammurabi was also engraved in stone sometime around 1750 BC. This code details 282 sections of how one individual should treat another individual in society and the penalties for such violations. The code is seen as the beginning of law and justice. Around 1000 BC, Mosaic Law emerged. This was a new form of rational law intended to predict prohibited behaviors.

In Mosaic Law, the ruling class did not create the law. The Code of Hammurabi and Mosaic Law formed the ladder that would eventually lead to the creation of policing as we now know it today (Berg, 1999).

Peisistratus (605-527 BC), the ruler of Athens, has been called the father of formal policing. During this time of growth, new Greek city-states were being developed, and blood feuds that lasted decades had to be quashed. Kin policing slowly faded due to its barbaric nature, and new doors opened for a modern city-driven policing model. The first police service in Athens was developed by Sparta, and it is often looked at as the first secret service (Berg, 1999).

Augustus Caesar (27 BC), the first emperor of Rome, was instrumental in creating what is now called the urban cohorts. The urban cohorts were men from the Praetorian Guard (Augustus' army), charged with ensuring peace in the city. As crime rose and became more violent, Augustus formed the vigils, which were not affiliated with the Praetorian Guard, but were charged with fighting crime and fires. The vigils were given the power to protect and arrest (Berg, 1999). From 6 A.D. until the 12th century, Rome was patrolled day and night by a public police force. With the fall of the Roman Empire, kings then assumed the role of protection. From the 12th to the 18th centuries, kings in England appointed sheriffs. At age fifteen, boys could volunteer for the posse comitatus to pursue wanted felons. Constables, policemen with limited authority, assisted sheriffs in serving summonses and warrants. Since young volunteers handled the policing, several problems arose, including corruption and drunkenness. Victims who had the means to hire private police or bodyguards did so for protection, but unfortunately, that meant those who were poor and disadvantaged had neither help nor protection (Berg, 1999) and thus were more of a target.

The 19th century in England heavily influenced the history of policing in the United States. Not only did policing change radically for the first time in over six centuries, but the father of modern policing, Sir Robert Peel (see figure 6.2), set the stage for what is known today as modern policing. Sir Robert Peel, the British Home Secretary, coined the term "bobbies" as a nickname for policemen, and he believed policing needed to be restructured.

In 1829, he passed the Metropolitan Police Act, which created the first British police force and what the 21st century now knows as modern-day police (Cordner et al., 2017). Sir Robert Peel is best known for the Peelian Principles. He did not create the twelve principles but used a combination of previous codes that he expected police to follow. The exact historical origins of the twelve listed principles below are unknown. Still, it has been theorized that the principles were slowly created over the years by academics studying Peel (Cordner et al., 2017): Peelian Principles.

- The police must be stable, efficient, and organized along military lines;
- The police must be under government control;
- The absence of crime will best prove the efficiency of the police;
- The distribution of crime news is essential;
- The deployment of police strength both by time and area is essential;
- No quality is more indispensable to a policeman than perfect command of temper;
- A quiet, determined manner has more effect than violent action;
- The securing and training of proper persons is at the root of efficiency;
- Public security demands that every police officer be given a number;
- Police headquarters should be centrally located and easily accessible to the people;
- Policemen should be hired on a probationary basis; and
- Police records are necessary for the proper allocation of police resources.

Policing Eras

With England's influence on the United States, much of the early history was shaped by what immigrants had experienced in their mother countries. These policing practices were passed down from generation to generation until political figures and policymakers in the United States began to make changes, shaping the progression of police reforms in the years and eras that followed. Researchers like Kelling and Moore (1991) evaluated the first three eras of policing in the United States. These eras are discussed in this section and are often referred to as the Political Era, the Reform Era, and the Community Era. These eras shaped how police forces were organized and their focus during specific time periods.

The Political Era

The political era is often referred to as the first era of policing in the United States. It began around the 1840s with the creation of the first Bonafede police agencies in America (Kelling et al, 1991). This era of policing was marked by the industrial revolution, the abolition of slavery, and the formation of large cities. With the advent of the industrial revolution came goods and services. Along with new job opportunities came a myriad of conflicts. With the abolishment of slavery, the Klu Klux Klan began to make terrifying appearances, and their reign of terror left many in fear. Policing had not yet formally entered the scene; therefore, the Klan operated virtually unencumbered. The fast-growing cities answered these problems in the form of policing. The United States saw tremendous growth in major cities, resulting in the creation of police departments across the United States in larger cities, as noted:

- The New York Police Department, founded in 1845
- The Chicago Police Department, founded in 1855
- The Philadelphia Police Department, founded in 1751
- The Jacksonville Police Department, founded in 1822
- The Detroit Police Department, founded in 1865
- The Portland Police Department, founded in 1870

With each of these three influences, the Political Era of policing was set into motion. As its name suggests, it was an era of politics, mainly because policing was limited by new laws mandated by the Constitution. America answered the call by following the English and Sir Robert Peel's principles. Not unlike today, policing during this era was under the control of politicians. Politicians, like the mayor, had no problem controlling everything a policeman did during his call of duty.

The Reform Era

Since the Political Era of policing ended up being laced with corruption and brutality, the panacea for the negativity became the Reform Era. One police chief was largely at the forefront of this new era, Chief August Vollmer. He is considered the pioneer of police professionalism. August Vollmer was the Chief of Police in Berkeley, California (1905–1932). He had many new beliefs about policing that would forever change the world of policing, including the following:

- Candidates who were testing to be in policing had to undergo psychological and intelligence tests.
- Detectives would utilize scientific methods in their investigations, through forensic laboratories.
- Recruits would, for the first time, attend a training academy (police had not received any formal training prior to August Vollmer's arrival).
- Assist with the development of the School of Criminology at the University of California, Berkeley.

Chief August Vollmer saw policing and officers as social workers who needed to delve into the causes of the acts to solve the issue, rather than just arrest them (Reppetto, 1978). He knew that to rehabilitate offenders, police officers needed to look beyond the handcuffs and examine the person and the reasons behind the behavior (Reppetto, 1978). Diversity in policing began to make a mark during this era, but it would fall far short of meeting any standard. It was a better era for diversity because agencies began hiring some women and people of varying races more than during the Political Era, but nowhere near the population ratios at the time.

The Community Era (1980s to 2000)

In the 1960s and 1970s, the crime rate doubled, and it was a time of unrest and eye-opening policing issues. Civil rights movements spread across America, and the police were on the front lines. Media coverage showed controversial contact between White male officers and Black community members, which further irritated race relations in policing. The US Supreme Court handed down the landmark Miranda v. Arizona and Mapp v. Ohio decisions. The writing was on the wall that the policing environment had to change. The days of answering everything with bullying or police professionalism were no more. The Community Era of policing began, and those in police administration hoped this new era would hold the answers to decades-old issues. The police needed help, so they turned to the community for assistance. This new era of community policing held that police could not act alone; the community must pitch in as well. Whether the problems were a dispute between neighbors or a high crime area, drugs and shootings, these issues did not develop overnight and could not be solved by a response of police alone. Instead, these community problems needed a pronged approach in which the police worked with the community, and over time, the issues could be systematically solved. Out-of-the-box thinking was common in community policing, and community leaders were often identified to make an impact. During this time, police candidates began appearing for the application process with Associate's and Bachelor's degrees. The "old school officers" mocked these degree-holding candidates, but the landscape was changing, and officers needed more thorough training than ever to answer the call.

Problem-oriented policing was an aftereffect of community policing, in that it used community policing but focused on problems first. The biggest difference was that problem-oriented policing used a defined process to work toward the solution. The problem was torn apart layer by layer and rebuilt according to set parameters that had a proven record of working. The Community Era was also a time for research. Prior to this era, research on crime, police, and criminal justice topics was scarce. With new federal government funding options available, this era's missions could be accomplished through grants, and the needed research began. Proof of what worked and what did not, along with suggestions for improving policing, was abundant. Without research or studies, policing can become stagnant, but with funding available, the answers were a questionnaire or interview away, and solutions came rolling in.

The Homeland Security Era (2001 to Present)

On September 11, 2001, when terrorists hijacked airplanes and flew them into the World Trade Center buildings and Pentagon in the United States, a fourth era of policing, the era of Homeland Security, was said to emerge (Oliver, 2006). The long-lasting repercussions of this terrorist act would forever change life for Americans. The realities of the tragedy of 9/11 were that it did start a new era of policing. In fact, a case could be made for the large dark line that became metaphorically visible on September 11, 2001, when the Community Era shifted to the Homeland Security Era as airplanes destroyed America's feelings of safety. Although the focus shifted to Homeland Security, policing has continued to involve some Community Era policing components. Policing under Homeland Security was marked by a more focused concentration of resources on crime control, enforcement of criminal law, traffic law, and related areas to expose potential threats and gather intelligence (Oliver, 2006). Scholars have examined the pros and cons of a national police department in the United States. For example, Canada has a Royal Canadian Mounted Police. Depending on the location, one could drive through several cities and counties on the way to the store, each with its own police department. With the advent of the Homeland Security Era, a new model of centralized organizational control began due to the need for information dissemination. One of the biggest flaws of 9/11 was the lack of communication between law enforcement agencies. The Department of Homeland Security was established, and one of its first major missions became disseminating information and communicating. While a national police department does not exist in the United States, communication and information are now common threads that bind the different types of law enforcement agencies.

Racialized and Biased History

As mentioned previously in the policing eras of the United States, law enforcement and minority groups have a rocky past, but this past started even before the policing eras began. The NAACP's website titled, The Origins of Modern Day Policing, explains that in the early 1700s, "Slave Patrols" were established in which white men were used to "establish a system of terror and squash slave uprisings with the capacity to pursue, apprehend and return runaway slaves to their owners. Tactics included the use of excessive force to control and produce desired slave behavior." (2021). The article goes on to explain that, "Slave Patrols continued until the end of the Civil War and the passage of the 13th Amendment. Following the Civil War, during Reconstruction, slave patrols were replaced by militia-style groups who were empowered to control and deny access to equal rights to freed slaves. They relentlessly and systematically enforced Black Codes, strict local and state laws that regulated and restricted access to labor, wages, voting rights, and general freedoms for formerly enslaved people." (NAACP, 2021)

The Black Codes continued to be enforced up until 1868, when the 14th Amendment of the Constitution was ratified, thus abolishing these codes, but in response individual states and local governments began passing Jim Crow laws, legalizing segregation in public places. With the creation of police departments, as noted in the political era, it became the role of policemen to enforce the Jim Crow Laws, which were in place until the 1960s (NAACP, 2021). To learn more about Jim Crow Laws, review Before the 1960s, as long as an individual was a white male, police officer positions were his for the taking. Women and minorities were all but non-existent on the force. Women were allowed into the "boys only club" if they wore a pencil skirt and fit a prescribed role consistent with being a woman. In some departments, women were allowed to work in the detective bureau and interview child victims because women supposedly talked to children better than men, because of their "maternal" instincts. These stereotypes continued in policing towards women and minorities until new laws forbidding such behavior made their way onto the scene. With new employment laws enacted between the 1960s and the late 1990s, many doors opened for women and minorities interested in becoming police officers.

Philosophy vs. Programs

Community policing is fundamentally a philosophy and an organizational strategy that redefine the role of police, moving beyond a series of standalone programs or a "one-size-fits-all" approach. The key distinction lies in its holistic nature and core principle of police-citizen partnerships. Community policing is a core belief system that drives all aspects of police work, from hiring and training to daily operations and performance measures. It is a long-term, fundamental institutional change centered on the idea that the police and public must work together as partners to identify and solve problems of crime and disorder. Treating community policing merely as a set of programs (like "Neighborhood Watch" or specific community meetings) often leads to failure or limited success because the underlying organizational culture and mission do not change. These programs, while valuable, are just tools for implementing the broader philosophy, not the philosophy itself.

The US Department of Justice Office of Community Oriented Policing Services (COPS) outlines three core components: This is the heart of the philosophy, involving collaborative relationships between law enforcement agencies and the individuals and organizations they serve (businesses, non-profits, media, etc.). The goal is to build mutual trust and a shared sense of responsibility for public safety. The philosophy requires a shift across the entire police agency's structure, management, personnel, and information systems to proactively support community engagement. This means moving away from a command-and-control model to one that empowers line officers with more decision-making authority.

Instead of a reactive, incident-driven approach, community policing uses systematic problem-solving techniques (such as the SARA model: Scanning, Analysis, Response, Assessment) to address the underlying conditions that cause public safety issues, rather than just the symptoms. Community policing is an integrated and comprehensive approach that aims to embed police within the community they serve, fostering trust and collaboration for long-term solutions, rather than short-term fixes offered by isolated programs.

Core Components of Community Policing

Community policing is generally built around three core components (often referred to as pillars or principles): Community Partnerships, Organizational Transformation, and Problem Solving. This involves collaborating with community members, local government agencies, non-profits, businesses, and other stakeholders to develop solutions to problems and increase trust in law enforcement. This includes ongoing communication to bring in public viewpoints and build mutually beneficial relationships. This component requires aligning the police agency's management structure, personnel, and information systems to support community partnerships and proactive problem-solving efforts. This often involves changes in training, performance evaluations, and the overall organizational culture to be more responsive and accountable to the public. Police engage in the proactive and systematic examination of identified problems to develop and evaluate effective responses. This moves beyond simply responding to calls for service to addressing the underlying causes of crime and disorder. A common model for this is the SARA process (Scanning, Analysis, Response, and Assessment). These components work together to create a more effective, responsive, and community-oriented approach to policing, ultimately enhancing public safety and community well-being.

Strategies to Build Trust and Legitimacy

Building trust and legitimacy is a core pillar of community policing that involves fostering positive, non-enforcement interactions between officers and the public to create a more cooperative relationship. This can be achieved through strategies such as community policing visits, which aim to improve residents' attitudes toward police and their willingness to cooperate, and by emphasizing procedural justice and the fair use of force in all police interactions. Encourage officers to engage the public in positive, non-enforcement ways, such as through door-to-door community visits. Ensure that police practices are perceived as fair. This includes treating people with respect, giving them a voice in decisions, being neutral in decision-making, and being transparent and honest.

Actively work to reduce the instances of excessive force, as this is a key factor in eroding public trust and legitimacy. Work with the community to solve problems and address concerns, fostering greater mutual understanding and trust.

Impact of Building Trust and Legitimacy

Studies show that positive contact with police can substantially improve residents' attitudes toward the police, including feelings of legitimacy and a greater willingness to cooperate. A more trusting relationship between the police and the community makes residents more likely to share information and assist in criminal investigations. When the community trusts the police, it can lead to greater cooperation and more effective crime reduction strategies, as the public becomes a more active partner.

Policy: Defining the Philosophy and Strategy

Community policing policies emphasize a law enforcement philosophy that promotes partnerships between the police and the community to solve problems and prevent crime, while oversight structures ensure accountability and public trust. Policy and oversight are interconnected: policies define the principles of community policing (partnership, problem-solving, prevention), and oversight mechanisms provide accountability to ensure these policies are implemented effectively and address community concerns.

Partnership

Community policing is a philosophy that holds that police and citizens should work together creatively to address community issues such as crime, social disorder, and neighborhood decay. It shifts from a reactive model to a proactive one, focusing on addressing the root causes of crime and public safety issues rather than just responding to incidents. Policies often involve implementing proactive measures, such as neighborhood watch groups, community meetings, and outreach activities, to prevent crime before it occurs. It requires the community to have a say in shaping local law enforcement priorities and working with police to build a safer environment.

Mechanisms

Oversight can include citizen police oversight boards or commissions, which are often created to ensure accountability and help rebuild trust between the police and the community.

The goal is to hold the police accountable for their actions and to provide a channel for community feedback and concerns, ensuring they are serving the public effectively. Effective oversight helps ensure that the police's actions align with the community's interests and are implemented in a way that fosters mutual trust and respect.

Examples: The creation of a policing oversight board in Southwark, London, was a direct response to a review that highlighted significant failings and called for rebuilding trust with the community.

Policy is the "What" and "How": Policies set the goals and methods for community policing, such as building partnerships and solving problems proactively. Oversight ensures that the policies are being followed, that the police are accountable to the community, and that the implementation of community policing is effective and fair. Effective policies, when coupled with strong oversight, can create a positive cycle in which increased trust enables better policy implementation, which, in turn, improves public safety and strengthens the relationship between the police and the community.

Technology and social media are used in community policing. Technology and social media are used to enhance community policing by improving communication, increasing transparency, and fostering collaboration between the police and the citizens. They enable real-time information sharing, citizen reporting, and the dissemination of crime-prevention tips through platforms such as social media, community engagement apps, and direct messaging. This approach helps build trust and can be used for intelligence gathering, investigations, and public outreach. Police departments use social media for direct and real-time communication with the public, sharing information and advice instantly. Social media platforms and community apps can be used for public outreach, allowing citizens to report incidents, provide feedback, and participate in solving local problems. Social media monitoring can help police identify potential threats, gather real-time intelligence, and respond to issues proactively. By actively engaging online, police can foster a sense of trust and transparency within the community. For example, they can share updates, respond to public concerns, and acknowledge citizen input. Apps and platforms allow citizens to report incidents, suspicious behavior, or other issues directly to the police, often with location and media attachments, resulting in faster response times. Police use social media and apps to provide immediate public notifications about safety concerns, such as local crime alerts or missing persons, keeping the community informed and engaged.

The spread of fake news and rumors on social media can undermine community policing efforts. Police may face challenges with abusive comments and the need to monitor and manage online interactions appropriately. To be effective, community policing through technology requires clear policies, training for officers, and a strong framework for use. The success of these tools relies on mutual trust, clear guidelines, and active participation from both citizens and law enforcement. The component of community policing focuses on joint problem-solving, building trust, and addressing the root causes of crime, rather than just reacting to incidents. Benefits include improved crime prevention, better community-police relations, and a stronger sense of neighborhood well-being. Police and community members work together to identify local problems, such as specific crime hotspots or areas of disorder, and create tailored solutions. Fostering strong relationships allows for greater information sharing, as residents feel more comfortable reporting suspicious activity to the police. Police departments adapt their structures, training, and management to support partnerships, which may include a focus on proactive problem-solving. The community's role includes participating in initiatives like neighborhood watch programs, attending meetings, and collaborating with schools and local groups.

By addressing root causes and implementing proactive measures, these partnerships can lead to a reduction in crime. When police and community members work together, they can create a safer environment for everyone. The approach shifts from a traditional, reactive model to a more collaborative one, improving trust and communication. When residents are involved in creating solutions, they develop a greater sense of ownership and investment in their neighborhood's safety. Officer training and wellness are crucial to community policing, with wellness training focusing on physical and mental health, and on trauma to manage the stress of law enforcement. Community policing skills, such as communication, empathy, and problem-solving, are essential for officers to build trust and collaborate effectively with the community. Training must integrate these areas, preparing officers for both their public-facing roles and the personal toll these duties take. This includes mandatory physical fitness programs, nutrition, and stress reduction techniques. Training is provided to help officers deal with the psychological impact of their work and build peer support skills to intervene in mental health crises. Programs focus on preventing suicide and helping officers recover from the chronic stress and trauma of their job, including a specific focus on topics like moral injury and dealing with threats. Developing strong communication, empathy, and problem-solving skills is vital for building relationships and trust with community members. Training in community-oriented policing helps officers collaborate effectively with the community. Officers must be equipped to work with community members to solve problems collaboratively rather than solely relying on enforcement. A well-rested, mentally healthy officer is better equipped to use their communication and empathy skills to engage the community positively. By addressing the high-stress nature of policing through wellness training, officers can be less reactive and more proactive in community interactions. Officers who are both well-trained in community engagement and personally well are more likely to build the trust necessary for effective community policing efforts.

SARA Model Steps

Problem-Oriented Policing (POP) uses the SARA model—Scanning, Analysis, Response, and Assessment—as a central method to address the underlying causes of crime within a community policing framework. This proactive approach shifts from reacting to incidents to systematically identifying, analyzing, and solving persistent problems by developing and evaluating targeted solutions in collaboration with the community.

Scanning: Identify and prioritize persistent problems that cause harm to the community and require police attention. This involves gathering information to define the problem in specific detail (who, what, when, where, and why).

Analysis: Examine the causes, conditions, and contributing factors that allow the problem to persist. This step goes beyond the incident itself to understand the root causes. Develop and implement a customized strategy to address the identified problem. This phase may involve a wide range of innovative approaches and collaborative efforts with community partners to find effective solutions. Evaluate the effectiveness of the implemented response to determine if the problem was removed, reduced, or unintentionally worsened. This includes gathering feedback to inform future adjustments.

Effective community engagement involves strategies such as neighborhood watch programs, which foster collaboration on crime prevention, and police-community committees that facilitate dialogue and partnerships between the public and law enforcement. Police Community Support Officers (PCSOs) are also crucial, acting as visible, accessible figures to build trust and address local concerns directly. These initiatives build stronger community relationships, improve public safety, and help identify community needs that can be addressed through joint efforts.

Neighborhood Watch Programs

These programs empower residents to work with the police by being extra eyes and ears, reporting suspicious activity, and collaborating to create a safer environment.

Police-Community Committees

These formal or informal groups provide a structured platform for two-way communication. They allow residents and police to discuss local issues, share perspectives, and develop joint solutions to problems, fostering trust and mutual understanding.

Role of Police Community Support Officers (PCSOs)

PCSOs are a key part of community policing. They are non-sworn officers who are highly visible and accessible in the community. Their role includes:

- Building relationships with residents.
- Addressing local issues, such as anti-social behavior and minor offenses.
- Acting as a link between the community and the police.
- Providing a consistent police presence in specific neighborhoods.

Beyond structured programs, police can use a variety of methods, such as community events, public forums, and online platforms to raise awareness, promote inclusion, and build partnerships. When communities and police work together, crime often decreases, and a greater sense of security emerges.

Direct, positive interactions can significantly increase trust between community members and the police. These efforts help strengthen the social bonds within a community, making it more resilient. By understanding local needs directly, police can tailor their strategies more effectively to solve problems.

Police Culture Resistance

Implementing police body cameras involves several significant challenges and criticisms, including institutional resistance, issues of equitable application, and ongoing debate over their effectiveness in achieving desired outcomes. A major source of resistance among officers stems from the feeling of constant monitoring by their own superiors, which can be a significant source of stress and lead to higher rates of burnout. Officers may worry that footage will be used to nitpick their performance or lead to disciplinary actions for using "strong language" or employing necessary, but potentially criticizable, tactics. This can cause them to become overly cautious or legalistic, potentially hampering their ability to take control of situations effectively (a "de-policing" effect). Officers have concerns about their own privacy, such as personal conversations with colleagues being recorded or accidental recording in private settings, like during lunch or in the bathroom. They also express a need to protect police tactics, such as interactions with informants, which can be jeopardized if footage is made public. Police unions have, in some cases, proven to be an obstacle to the adoption of body cameras, often negotiating for procedural protections that can limit accountability and transparency.

Potential for Unequal Treatment

When officers have discretion over when to turn cameras on or off, it can lead to selective recording, potentially capturing only parts of an interaction that favor the officer's perspective. Restricting officer discretion in activation is suggested as a way to mitigate this. There are significant concerns about recording interactions with vulnerable individuals, such as victims of domestic violence or sexual assault, children, or those experiencing mental health crises. The fear is that being recorded might discourage victims from reporting crimes or providing full statements. While some studies suggest cameras can reduce racial disparities in "unstained" complaints, the interpretation of footage can still be subjective, and critics point out that outcomes for victims of police violence are not always guaranteed to result in accountability, with footage often delayed, redacted, or not released publicly.

Debate over Effectiveness

Mixed Results: Research findings on the effectiveness of body cameras are highly variable and inconsistent. While some studies show a reduction in citizen complaints, others find no clear or consistent effects on officer use of force, arrests, or citizen behavior. It is often unclear why certain effects occur, such as a drop in complaints. It could be due to improved officer behavior, or simply to the fact that citizens are deterred from filing complaints by the presence of video evidence.

Unintended Consequences

Some studies have reported unintended negative consequences, such as an increase in assaults against officers wearing cameras in certain contexts. Body camera programs are expensive, not just for the equipment but also for data storage, management, and administration. The lack of consistent evidence for clear benefits raises questions about their cost-effectiveness.

Case Study-1

Kansas City Preventive Patrol Experiment (US,1972-1973)

Community policing initiatives vary widely by location, influenced by local culture, existing police structures, and specific community needs. Key case studies demonstrate the diverse approaches and outcomes of these programs: This landmark experiment challenged the core assumption that routine, random preventive patrol deters crime. Across 15 police beats, patrol levels varied: some had normal patrol, some had doubled ("proactive") patrol, and some had no routine patrol (only reactive responses to calls). The study found no significant differences across the areas in crime rates (including violent, burglary, and larceny), citizens' fear of crime, citizens' attitudes toward police services, or police response time. The results indicated that traditional preventive patrol was not an effective use of police resources, leading to a major re-evaluation of policing strategies and providing impetus for developing more targeted approaches, such as community policing and data-driven "hot spots" policing.

Case Study-2
Programs in Chicago (US)

Chicago's Alternative Policing Strategy (CAPS) began in 1993, expanding citywide by 1995, and is a comprehensive, system-wide community policing philosophy. Key features include police-community beat meetings (which had stable attendance of around 6,000 persons per month in the late 90s and early 2000s), problem-solving techniques, and community partnerships to identify and address local issues. Evaluations showed that the program positively influenced public satisfaction with police services and improved police-citizen interaction, especially through informal, non-enforcement contacts. Perceptions of community policing had strong positive effects on satisfaction with police and crime prevention behaviors, although the direct impact on fear of crime was less clear.

Case Study-3
Programs in India

India has seen various community policing initiatives across different states, often operating under different names, to bridge the significant trust gap between the public and the police. Examples include:

Friends of Police (FOP) in Tamil Nadu: This organization involves citizens as partners in crime prevention and detection, thereby enhancing police-public relations.

Janamaithri Suraksha Project in Kerala: Credited with reducing crime rates and improving police-community relations through collaboration and legal awareness programs.

"Mohalla Committee Movement" in Mumbai and Pune: Formed after communal riots to maintain harmony and involve local residents in identifying potential triggers for unrest and solving local problems.

These initiatives have led to a significant reduction in crime rates in specific areas, increased public satisfaction and perceived safety, and enhanced public trust in the police. Challenges include resource constraints, institutional resistance, and the need for context-specific approaches.

Case Study-4
Programs in Canada

Community policing in Canada is often implemented through local agreements and community-based programs, particularly in Indigenous communities. Examples include the Royal Canadian Mounted Police's (RCMP) Community Tripartite Agreements (CTAs) and Aboriginal Community Constable Programs (ACCPs), designed to provide tailored policing services in collaboration with local governments and Indigenous communities. These programs highlight the need for tailored, local-level agreements to clarify roles and responsibilities and encourage greater cooperation. However, some earlier projects had uneven performance and faced criticism for reinforcing existing power hierarchies or having limited training on human rights issues.

Case Study-5

Programs in the UK

The UK has a history of community-oriented policing, stemming from the philosophy that "the police are the public, the public are the police". Modern initiatives often focus on neighborhood policing teams working with local residents and partners to address crime and disorder. Donor countries like the UK have also funded community policing initiatives in post-conflict and transitional countries, such as supporting basic police training in South Africa. UK policing of the "Irish problem" in the 19th century is a classic example of policing as social control, leading to over-policing of certain groups. Modern community policing efforts aim to move beyond this historical context, but, as in other countries, effectiveness depends heavily on local implementation and commitment to collaboration.

Technology and Data

Use these tools to predict crime hotspots and manage resources more efficiently. Employ AI-driven tools to enhance communication between police and citizens through social media and other digital platforms. Implement body-worn cameras and enhanced reporting systems to increase accountability.

Partnership and Collaboration

Broader Community Involvement: Move beyond police-community forums to create more inclusive partnerships and ensure that all voices are heard, particularly those of minority and vulnerable populations. Improve collaboration between local, state, and federal agencies to address complex crimes more effectively. Shift focus from solely law enforcement to working with social workers and other specialists to address issues like mental health and homelessness.

Prevention and Workforce Development

Preventive Measures: Focus on addressing root causes of crime, particularly among youth, through programs that promote positive development and reduce recidivism.

Emphasize conflict resolution and healing over punitive measures where appropriate.

Train officers with specialized knowledge in new technologies and cultural competence to work effectively in diverse environments.

Policy and Structure

Uniform Frameworks: Develop standardized, nationwide frameworks for community policing to ensure consistency and effectiveness, as a lack of uniformity has been a barrier in places like India. Drive internal cultural change within police departments to support community-oriented strategies and increase efficiency.

Contemporary Issues and Future Thinkers

Contemporary community policing is primarily a philosophy and organizational strategy that has been shaped by foundational figures and is evolving in response to modern challenges like technology, cybercrime, mental health crises, and the ongoing need to build community trust and legitimacy. The modern concept of community policing has been influenced by a number of key thinkers who have defined its principles and implementation:

Sir Robert Peel

The "father of modern policing," Sir Robert Peel, inhis early-19th-century "Peelian Principles," emphasized that "police, at all times, should seek to obtain the co-operation of the public" and that "police legitimacy" derives from public consent, a core tenet of community policing today.

James Q. Wilson and George Kelling
Their influential "Broken Windows" theory suggested that disorder and minor crimes, if left unchecked, lead to more serious crime, providing a theoretical underpinning for community order-maintenance approaches that rely on reinforcing informal community control mechanisms.

Robert Trojanowicz
Often referred to as the "father of community policing," he provided a roadmap for its implementation that has been extended by subsequent research and texts.

Victor E. Kappeler, Larry K. Gaines, and Brian P. Schaefer
The authors of *Community Policing: A Contemporary Perspective* are current educational and research figures who promote the understanding of community policing as a comprehensive philosophy rather than just a set of tactics.

Steven Herbert
He views community policing as a potentially fundamental, but difficult, change to traditional policing culture, highlighting the tension between the progressive ethos of shared governance and established police norms.

David Bayley
A critic by profession, he has raised concerns that implementing community policing policies might reduce crime-control effectiveness or lead to increased bureaucratic power, underscoring the ongoing debate over its practical application and outcomes.

Contemporary Issues
Police officers in the modern era face significant challenges that shape the future of community policing, including workforce and staffing shortages, the need to build community trust, and the rise of complex new crimes like cybercrime. To address these issues, law

enforcement is focusing on community-oriented policing strategies, implementing new technologies, and prioritizing officer health and wellness.

Technology and Cybercrime

The significant shift of crime to online platforms (with over 40% of all crime now being fraud) requires an "innovation revolution" in policing that traditional methods are not equipped to handle.

Mental Health Crises

Police are increasingly diverted by social problems, such as responding to mental health-related encounters, which consume significant resources and time.

Building and Maintaining Trust

Public confidence in policing has declined, and building trust and legitimacy, especially within minority communities, remains a central and difficult goal. The President's Task Force on 21st Century Policing identified "Building Trust and Legitimacy" as its primary pillar.

Staffing Shortages and Workloads

Many departments face large workloads and staff shortages, making it challenging to implement the resource-intensive, personalized service often required by the community policing model.

Defining and Measuring Success

There is no single, fixed definition of community policing, and research has found mixed results regarding the effectiveness of some programs in consistently reducing crime rates or police violence, leading to calls for better evaluation methodologies.

Future Directions

Future thinkers and approaches in community policing focus on several key areas, emphasizing the integration of traditional methods with modern challenges: Future policing will rely heavily on advanced technology, including artificial intelligence (AI), big data analytics, predictive policing, and integrated surveillance systems (drones, facial recognition, body-worn cameras). These tools will aid in crime prevention, resource allocation, and evidence management, making policing more data-driven and efficient. The next generation of community policing will shift toward a more strategic use of information and a proactive, problem-solving approach (such as the SARA model: Scanning, Analysis, Response, Assessment) to address the root causes of crime and disorder, moving away from purely reactive responses. Building and rebuilding public trust remains a critical component. Future efforts focus on transparent communication, increased officer accountability, and genuine collaboration with diverse community groups, non-profits, and other government agencies to co-produce public safety. Law enforcement will need to address complex issues such as cybercrime, mental health crises, and social problems. This requires officers with diverse skill sets (e.g., data scientists, social workers) and seamless collaboration among local, state, federal, and international agencies. The future workforce will require new skills, including digital competencies and emotional intelligence. There will be a focus on supporting officers' well-being and providing tailored training programs to prepare them for the complexities of modern, non-homogeneous communities. The increased use of data and technology necessitates strong ethical guidelines, privacy protections, and community oversight to ensure transparency, prevent bias, and maintain public confidence. In essence, the future of community policing involves a hybrid approach that combines human-centered engagement and problem-solving with the power of data and technology to create safer, more just communities.

Innovation and Adaptation

Experts like Simon O. Eller suggest that police organizations need to be highly adaptive and foster a "culture of innovation" to keep pace with a digitized society.

Data-Driven, Equitable Approaches

Future models emphasize leveraging technology while ensuring privacy and equity, focusing on addressing systemic biases in law enforcement through evidence-based strategies.

Focus on Core Functions

Some experienced police professionals argue that the future of policing should prioritize core functions such as responding to urgent calls and ensuring adequate staffing, potentially creating tension with the broader problem-solving mandate of community policing.

Integrative Thinking in Leadership

The future requires police leaders to be "integrative thinkers" who can welcome complexity and see how different parts of a problem fit together, generating new solutions in an environment with hard-to-measure outcomes.

Part I
The Foundations of the Philosophy

INTRODUCTION

The philosophical foundations of community policing were shaped by several key thinkers and researchers who advocated for a shift from the traditional, reactive model of policing to a proactive, community-centered approach. The core thinkers and their contributions include:

Sir Robert Peel: Although community policing is a modern term, its roots are often traced back to the principles established by Sir Robert Peel in 1829 when he founded the London Metropolitan Police. His core philosophy emphasized that "the police are the public and the public are the police" and that police legitimacy and effectiveness depend on public approval and cooperation, thereby laying an early foundation for community consent.

James Q. Wilson and George Kelling: Their influential 1982 article, "Broken Windows: The Police and the Neighborhood Safety," theorized that visible signs of crime, anti-social behavior, and civil disorder (e.g., broken windows, litter, graffiti) create an urban environment that encourages further crime and disorder. They argued that police should address these minor "quality of life" issues in partnership with the community to prevent more serious crimes, thereby directly influencing community policing's focus on neighborhood quality of life.

Herman Goldstein: He developed the concept of Problem-Oriented Policing (POP). Goldstein argued that the police should move away from simply responding to incidents (calls for service) and instead focus on identifying and analyzing the underlying causes of recurrent community problems. This systematic use of problem-solving techniques (often encapsulated by the SARA model: Scanning, Analysis, Response, Assessment) is a cornerstone of the community policing philosophy.

Robert Trojanowicz and Bonnie Bucqueroux: From the National Center for Community Policing at Michigan State

University, they provided a widely cited definition of community policing: "a new philosophy of policing, based on the concept that police officers and private citizens working together in creative ways can help solve contemporary community problems related to crime, social and physical disorder, and neighborhood decay". They stressed the importance of police officers being permanently assigned to specific beats to foster strong, lasting relationships with residents and businesses.

David Bayley: A notable scholar who has examined the concept and implementation of community policing internationally. While supportive of the philosophy, he has also raised critical questions about the challenges of implementing it effectively and ensuring it does not lead to unequal treatment or the erosion of civil liberties, offering an important perspective on its practical application. These thinkers helped establish the core tenets of community policing, which are:

- Partnerships: Building collaborative relationships with community members, local government agencies, and businesses.
- Problem-solving: Addressing the underlying causes of crime and other community issues rather than just reacting to individual incidents.
- Organizational change: Implementing decentralized authority, flexible organizational structures, and empowering frontline officers to make independent decisions tailored to local needs.
- Prevention: Emphasizing proactive crime prevention efforts over reactive responses.

Chapter 1 | THE TRADITIONAL ERA AND ITS DISCONTENTS

The objective of studying the pre-1970s policing model is to understand its inherent limitations, which ultimately led to a decline in public trust and highlighted the need for significant reform, paving the way for the community policing era. Before the 1970s, the dominant policing model, particularly during the "Reform Era" (roughly 1930s-1970s), emphasized professionalism, efficiency, and a centralized, reactive approach to crime. This model aimed to remove political corruption from policing, but it resulted in police becoming detached from their communities. James Q. Wilson, in his seminal 1968 work *Varieties of Police Behavior*, identified three distinct policing styles prevalent in different types of communities, each with its own focus and shortcomings:

Watchman Style: This style prioritized order maintenance through informal control and a high degree of officer discretion. Officers often ignored minor infractions to "keep the peace" by issuing threats or using persuasion. While seeking to resolve disputes informally, this approach often raised concerns about inequality and potential discrimination, as discretion could be applied inconsistently, particularly in low-income or ethnically diverse neighborhoods.

Legalistic Style: This style operated strictly "by the book," emphasizing formal law enforcement with minimal officer discretion. Every complaint was treated formally, resulting in high arrest and ticketing rates. This paramilitary approach, common in larger cities, fostered an impersonal relationship with the public and was perceived as rigid and disconnected from community needs.

Service Style: Found mainly in suburban, middle-class communities, this style focused on serving the public and helping the community through informal methods. While it emphasized public relations, it often prioritized the concerns of affluent residents over others and maintained a certain level of social homogeneity.

Need for Reform

The objective of studying these styles and the overall pre-1970s model is to examine the roots of policing's challenges: The detached and reactive nature of the reform model, coupled with high-profile violent clashes during the civil rights movement and urban riots of the 1960s, severely damaged the relationship and trust between police and many communities. Rising crime rates, despite the professional model's emphasis on rapid response and arrests, indicated that traditional methods were not sufficient to ensure public safety or prevent crime effectively. The one-way communication model and the focus on statistics (such as response times) neglected the importance of community input and cooperation in identifying and solving local problems. Ultimately, the study of the traditional era and its discontents serves to highlight the necessity of a paradigm shift towards the Community Era, where police work collaboratively with residents to identify the root causes of crime and disorder, rebuild trust, and share responsibility for public safety. Thinkers like Herman Goldstein and Robert Trojanowicz argued for this fundamental reorientation, advocating problem-oriented, community-focused strategies that moved beyond the limitations of traditional styles.

Watchman Style

The concept of the "watchman style" of policing was developed by the American political scientist James Q. Wilson in his seminal work, as one of three distinct approaches to police work (the others being the legalistic and service styles). The watchman style is a traditional approach to policing, primarily focused on maintaining public order and keeping the peace through informal methods. The primary goal is resolving disputes and addressing immediate consequences rather than strict, proactive law enforcement. Officers are given wide latitude in deciding which offenses to pursue, often overlooking minor offences in favor of the broader goal of stability. The seriousness of an offense is often judged by its immediate local impact, rather than a universal legal standard. Officers rely on warnings, mediation, and community ties rather than formal arrests or citations. This style was historically popular during the political era of policing and is often found in communities with a mix of ethnic populations and blue-collar or rural, small-town areas, possibly with limited resources.

Its Discontents and the Rise of Community Policing

The "discontents" of the watchman style, as referenced in your query, largely stem from its potential for inequality and discrimination. The wide discretion granted to officers can lead to: Decisions about who to arrest or warn can be perceived as unfair, particularly by minority groups, leading to concerns about police profiling. The informal nature of the work can clash with modern ideals of professional, impartial law enforcement that apply a single community standard. These issues, along with a broader call for police reform, contributed to the evolution of policing into the community era, which began around the 1980s. The community policing model was developed to counteract the limitations of both the watchman and legalistic styles by emphasizing:

- Fostering rapport and trust between officers and community members.
- Working with the community to address underlying problems that lead to crime, rather than just reacting to incidents.
- Encouraging community involvement in public safety efforts.

In essence, community policing thinkers sought a model that was more responsive and accountable to the public, moving beyond the sometimes arbitrary or informal nature of the traditional watchman approach.

The Legalistic Style of Policing

The legalistic style of policing is a formal, "by the book" approach that emphasizes strict adherence to the law and minimal officer discretion. This paramilitary model, often found in larger cities, treats every complaint formally, resulting in high arrest and ticketing rates [1]. Officers prioritize the technical letter of the law over situational nuances. This style results in high rates of formal actions, such as arrests and traffic citations. A rigid approach can create a perception of impersonality and disconnection from community needs [1]. This style stands in contrast to other models, such as the watchman style (emphasizing order maintenance and discretion) and the service style (focusing on community needs and problem-solving) [1].

The "Service Style" of Policing

The "Service Style" of policing is one of three key styles identified by James Q. Wilson in his seminal 1968 book *Varieties of Police Behavior*. This style is characterized by police prioritizing community needs and assistance over strict law enforcement, often using informal methods to resolve issues. Police in this style view themselves as helpers rather than just law enforcers, working to serve the public and assist community members with a variety of issues, not just crime. Officers exercise a significant amount of discretion, often issuing warnings or using persuasion to resolve disputes rather than making arrests or writing citations for minor infractions (e.g., warning speeding teenagers instead of ticketing them). This style is typically found in homogeneous, middle-class suburban communities with relatively low crime rates. Citizens in such areas often expect personalized and individual treatment from their police force. Departments employing this style often work with other social services and agencies to provide support and address underlying problems within the community. The provided description accurately notes that while this style emphasizes public relations and helping the community, it can implicitly favor the concerns of affluent residents and maintain social homogeneity, sometimes leading to disproportionate suspicion toward individuals from outside the community or minority groups.

Discontents of the "Traditional Era"

The chapter, "The Traditional Era and Its Discontents," by policing scholar David H. Bayley, critiques the limitations of conventional policing methods and argues for a shift towards community-oriented strategies. Bayley identified significant shortcomings in the traditional model of policing, which primarily emphasized a "reactive" approach based on motorized patrol, rapid response to calls for service, and post-crime investigations. The key discontents included: Research, most notably studies like the Kansas City Preventive Patrol Experiment, demonstrated that random preventive patrol had minimal impact on crime rates or citizen feelings of security. The remote, incident-driven nature of traditional policing often led to a disconnect and ingrained mistrust between law enforcement agencies and the communities they served, particularly non-white communities. Traditional policing primarily reacted to crime after it occurred, rather than addressing the underlying social problems and conditions that generate crime and disorder in the first place. The model often relied on a top-down, command-and-control structure, which could lead to an excessive or inappropriate use of force and a perception of unaccountability. The "Traditional Era" is not a single, universally defined historical period but a general term for pre-modern societies, characterized by ascribed, hierarchical leadership, an emphasis on duty to society over individual will, and economies often centered on resource exploitation. Leadership was generally ascribed (inherited or based on caste/status), rather than achieved through merit or election. This rigid structure led to significant power imbalances and social stratification. Societies prioritized conformity to divine or predetermined social codes and duties. Personal "self-will" or the creation of an individual identity was often seen as a problem, leading to a suppression of individual aspirations and autonomy. Early laws and systems during periods such as the rise of industrialization and colonialism were often designed to secure the commercial exploitation of natural resources for the benefit of colonial and capitalist societies, with little regard for intrinsic environmental values or local communities' rights. The existence of old-fashioned dictatorships and the lack of mechanisms to meet popular demands meant that citizens often lived under regimes where they had little say in their governance, leading to a desire to avoid tyranny. In non-Western contexts, "modernization" was often imposed by colonial powers, who sought to erase local culture and replace traditional beliefs and practices with Western templates. This imposition from above led to significant cultural and political conflict and to a failure to gain the people's confidence. In many traditional settings, women were educated to accept and believe in a prescribed, subordinate role within marriage and society, leading to discontent as modern ideas challenged these norms.

These discontents eventually contributed to social movements and transitions towards modernity, which promised greater individual self-direction, more representative political systems, and social justice, though the transition itself brought new tensions.

James Q. Wilson and Policing Styles

The concept of distinct policing styles, including the legalistic style, was developed by James Q. Wilson. In contrast to the legalistic style, community policing is a philosophy that emerged from thinkers like Herman Goldstein (who developed Problem-Oriented Policing, a precursor) and was promoted by figures such as David Bayley and Lee Brown. In his influential 1968 work, James Q. Wilson identified three primary styles of policing based on environmental demands and managerial preferences:

Watchman Style: It emphasizes order maintenance through informal methods and officer discretion, often found in rural or blue-collar communities.

Legalistic Style: It focuses on strict enforcement of the letter of the law, using formal methods like arrests and citations with little discretion. It is often described as a "paramilitary" style and is common in larger, ethnically diverse cities.

Service Style: It prioritizes serving the public and helping the community through informal methods and frequent interaction, typically in suburban, middle-class communities with low crime rates.

Thinker's Conclusion and Future Direction

Bayley's central conclusion was that the traditional policing paradigm was fundamentally inadequate for effectively ensuring public safety and maintaining legitimacy in a diverse, modern society. He argued for a radical shift towards community policing (or problem-oriented policing) as the necessary future direction. The traditional approach, while perhaps appearing efficient on paper, failed to deliver on its core promise of public safety and eroded public confidence. The future of policing lies in proactive engagement with communities to identify and solve specific problems. This involves developing collaborative, problem-solving partnerships with residents and local organizations; empowering frontline officers with the discretion and resources to address local concerns; prioritizing the building of trust and legitimacy as essential components of police effectiveness.

Bayley's work has been highly influential, serving as a cornerstone for the community policing movement and a catalyst for police reform worldwide. His arguments helped provide the intellectual justification for a shift in police strategy, emphasizing that police need the consent and cooperation of the governed to be truly effective. Some critics argue that true community policing is difficult to implement in practice, often becoming a superficial public relations exercise rather than genuine structural reform. The shift to problem-solving and community engagement can be resource-intensive and may require significant changes to police training and organizational structure. Questions remain about the appropriate role of the police in addressing complex social problems, which may require interventions from other social services.

Chapter 2 | THE ROOTS OF MODERN COMMUNITY POLICING

Robert Peel

Robert Peel was 62 when he died. He had sat in the Commons for more than 40 years and had held high office many times. As Home Secretary in 1829, he had created the 'Peelers' or 'Bobbies', the country's first efficient police force. He had served twice as prime minister, in 1834-35 and in 1841-46, and had broken his own Tory Party twice, in 1829 and again in 1846, after which he had supported the Whigs. Robert Peel's main contributions include founding the modern British police force, the Metropolitan Police, in 1829, and establishing the principles that guide it. He also served twice as Prime Minister and was a key figure in founding the modern Conservative Party, shaping 19th-century political stability and liberalism through his various policies, including introducing liberal measures while in government.

Founding the Metropolitan Police

As Home Secretary, Peel established the Metropolitan Police in 1829, creating a model for organized, modern policing in Britain and worldwide. He is associated with establishing a set of principles for the police that emphasize public cooperation, the use of force as a last resort, and the idea that police are the public and the public are the police. He defined police efficiency as the absence of crime and disorder, not the visible evidence of police action. Peel served twice as Prime Minister of the United Kingdom (1834–1835 and 1841–1846). He was one of the founders of the modern Conservative Party. He promoted a series of liberal measures in government that helped bridge political divides and contributed to the era's stability and prosperity. He served as Chancellor of the Exchequer from 1834 to 1835.

Introduction

This chapter on "The Roots of Modern Community Policing (Robert Peel)" aims to explain the historical basis of contemporary law enforcement, emphasize the need for public cooperation, and apply core principles to current policing issues. Key learning outcomes include understanding the origin of modern policing with Sir Robert Peel, defining the Peelian Principles such as crime prevention and policing by consent, analyzing their relevance to modern community policing, and evaluating contemporary challenges in adapting these principles. Sir Robert Peel was a British statesman known for his pivotal role in establishing modern policing through the creation of the Metropolitan Police Service in 1829. His innovative approach to law enforcement emphasized crime prevention, community cooperation, and the ethical conduct of police officers, laying the groundwork for contemporary police organizations. Sir Robert Peel is recognized as a foundational figure in modern policing and community policing due to his establishment of the London Metropolitan Police Force and his principles emphasizing police-public cooperation. His concept of "policing by consent" centered on the idea that police legitimacy and effectiveness rely on public approval and a partnership approach to safety. For more information, Sir Robert Peel is often referred to as the 'father of modern policing' due to his significant contributions to law enforcement practices. The Metropolitan Police Service was formed with the aim of reducing crime through proactive measures rather than simply responding to criminal incidents. Peel's vision for policing involved officers acting as public servants rather than military forces, promoting a more community-oriented approach. The Peelian Principles emphasize the importance of public cooperation in effective policing, highlighting that police derive their authority from public consent. Peel's reforms have influenced policing worldwide, leading to the establishment of similar forces in other countries based on his model.

How Did Sir Robert Peel's Establishment of the Metropolitan Police Service Change the Approach to Law Enforcement during His Time?

Sir Robert Peel's creation of the Metropolitan Police Service marked a significant shift in law enforcement from reactive measures to proactive crime prevention. By establishing a structured police force that focused on community engagement and public cooperation, Peel set a precedent for modern policing. This change aimed to address the root causes of crime rather than merely responding to incidents, fundamentally transforming how society viewed and interacted with law enforcement.

Discuss the Key Elements of the Peelian Principles and Their Significance in Modern Policing

The Peelian Principles outline essential ethical standards for police officers, emphasizing the importance of public cooperation and accountability. Key elements include the idea that police must maintain public trust to be effective and that their authority comes from community consent. These principles are significant because they laid a foundational philosophy for modern policing, guiding contemporary practices that prioritize transparency, ethics, and collaboration with communities.

Evaluate How Sir Robert Peel's Influence Can Be Seen in Contemporary Policing Strategies, such as Community Policing

Sir Robert Peel's influence is evident in contemporary policing strategies such as community policing, which emphasizes building strong relationships between police officers and community members. His belief in proactive crime prevention and ethical conduct has been integrated into modern approaches that involve officers engaging with citizens to address concerns collectively. This evaluation shows how Peel's vision continues to shape law enforcement practices today, fostering a collaborative environment focused on reducing crime and improving public safety, and highlighting the historical context and foundational principles of "the police are the public and the public are the police".

Historical Basis of Contemporary Law Enforcement

The focus on Robert Peel and the roots of community policing will cover the historical origins of modern law enforcement, the importance of public cooperation, and the application of Peel's core principles to contemporary issues. It aims to explain the historical basis of law enforcement by highlighting Peel's influence, emphasizing the need for public cooperation by linking it to his philosophy of policing by consent, and applying these core principles to current policing challenges. Robert Peel is considered the father of modern British policing for his role in establishing the Metropolitan Police in 1829. His principles laid the groundwork for modern police forces, emphasizing that the "power of the police is dependent on public approval". This historical basis is crucial for understanding how contemporary law enforcement has evolved and what foundational ideas guide its operations.

Ancient and Medieval Systems

Contemporary law enforcement's historical basis lies in the shift from informal, community-based systems to formalized, state-controlled police forces, most notably with the 19th-century London Metropolitan Police model. Early societies relied on informal or community-based systems for order.

Ancient Civilizations: Evidence from ancient Egypt around 3,000 BCE indicates that pharaoh's officials were responsible for public safety. In the Roman Empire, a variety of civilian and military groups handled order, but "self-help" among citizens was vital.

English Roots: Medieval England used the frankpledge system, which made all adult males collectively responsible for each other's conduct, formalized in groups called tithings. This evolved into the parish constable system, where local constables and watchmen, often unpaid or of low status, were tasked with maintaining order.

The Rise of Modern Policing

The 18th and 19th centuries, marked by urbanization and social unrest, necessitated a more organized approach to law enforcement. In mid-18th-century London, magistrates Henry Fielding and his brother, Sir John Fielding, improved policing by deploying select, paid constables as "pursuers" to disrupt criminal gangs.

- **The Peelian Principles:** Sir Robert Peel, the British Home Secretary, established the London Metropolitan Police with the Metropolitan Police Act of 1829. This force is considered the first modern police department and was built on principles that still influence policing today, including: The primary object of the police is the prevention of crime by a visible presence.
- **Policing by Consent:** Police power is dependent on public approval and cooperation.
- **Impartiality:** Police should provide neutral service to the law.
- **Minimal Force:** Physical force should only be used as a last resort.
- **Police Are the Public:** Police officers are members of the public who are paid to give full-time attention to the community's well-being.

Influence and Evolution in Other Regions

The London model heavily influenced law enforcement globally, though local contexts shaped its implementation:

The United States: Early American colonies had informal systems like night watches and slave patrols. The London model inspired the creation of the first municipal police departments in cities such as Boston, New York, and Philadelphia in the mid-19th century. Over time, American policing evolved through the professionalism era (early-mid 20th century) to modern community and problem-oriented policing strategies.

India: The British in India developed a policing system based on the Police Act of 1861, drawing on pre-existing Mughal structures but modeling the organization after the Irish Constabulary. This system established a provincial police force with a military structure designed to maintain colonial authority and control the populace, a legacy that continues to influence modern Indian policing and ongoing reform efforts. Today, while rooted in these historical models, contemporary law enforcement emphasizes community relations, human rights, and the use of technology to address modern crime and societal needs.

Need for Public Cooperation

The core of the historical argument is that police legitimacy and effectiveness depend on the public's trust and cooperation, a philosophy known as the consent model. Peel's famous quote, "the police are the people and the people are the police," encapsulates this idea of a symbiotic relationship between the two. The chapter will emphasize that this cooperation is not a choice but a necessity for successful law enforcement. Public cooperation is essential for effective public administration and services, as it leads to better-informed and more sustainable decisions through diverse perspectives. It also builds public trust, ensures policies are implemented more effectively, and helps government agencies operate efficiently. Public cooperation is vital for everything from providing essential services to ensuring national security. Public participation provides decision-makers with more information, values, and perspectives, leading to more complete and informed outcomes. Decisions are more likely to succeed when stakeholders understand the results and are invested in them. This is especially true for marginalized groups whose needs might otherwise be overlooked. Collaboration between the public and government fosters transparency and builds trust, which is crucial for effective governance. Cooperation ensures that government programs and services meet the needs of the public they are intended to serve. Cooperation is vital to the effective functioning of public administration, including services such as healthcare, transportation, and national defence, which are deemed too important to be left solely to private profit motives.

How Public Cooperation Is Achieved

The government can involve the public in decision-making through forums, feedback sessions, and other avenues for input. Strong public relations efforts by the government can foster communication and transparency, encouraging cooperation. These entities are specifically created to deliver essential services to the public and are a key mechanism for government investment in public goods.

Application to Current Policing Issues

The chapter will bridge the past and the present by demonstrating how these historical principles apply to modern policing. By examining Peel's foundational ideas, the chapter will explore how they can be applied to contemporary challenges in policing, such as building community trust and improving accountability. This application is essential for addressing current policing issues by applying timeless principles to new contexts and problems. Applications to current policing issues include technology such as AI-driven analytics and data portals, community-focused strategies such as community policing and beat officer systems to build trust, and modernized training that emphasizes de-escalation and human rights. There is also a strong push for scientific and data-driven approaches, including "hot spot" policing and advanced investigative tools, to improve efficiency and reduce reliance on traditional, sometimes coercive, methods.

Technology and Data-driven Solutions

The use of AI to help officers analyze vast amounts of data, identify crime trends, visualize hotspots, and generate actionable insights without advanced coding skills is explained on a national portal for citizens to report cybercrimes and receive assistance. An online platform should be there for citizens to file complaints, get information on FIRs, and access other police-related services. Tools like the CitizenCOP mobile app can provide citizens with an additional way to report issues and access information. BPR&D can help control violent crime, though its effectiveness and equity need ongoing evaluation.

Community and Trust-building Initiatives

There should be a direct engagement between law enforcement and local communities to build relationships and foster accountability. Assigning officers to specific beats to address local concerns, as seen in states like Maharashtra, can improve community relations. Regular public forums and outreach programs are needed to improve relations with marginalized communities. Staffing police stations with professionals is necessary to help handle sensitive cases like domestic violence and juvenile crimes.

Modernized Training and Procedures

The focus should be on social interaction skills, respect, and de-escalation, with examples from Finland and Rajasthan demonstrating positive impacts on public satisfaction. An evidence-based strategy is needed to identify the root causes of crime and disorder, though its full implementation can be challenging. Integrating more scientific methods can reduce the need for coercive practices. Training that emphasizes human rights norms and impartiality should be provided, as the Model Police Act highlights.

Transparency and Accountability

Installing cameras in police stations to deter misconduct and ensure fair treatment. Developing standard operating procedures (SOPs) and ensuring officers follow them, while also modernizing police policies. Proactively working with the media to share success stories and clarify public misunderstandings.

Conclusion on Robert Peel's Principles

Sir Robert Peel's principles remain the philosophical foundation for modern democratic policing, particularly the model of "policing by consent," which posits that police legitimacy and effectiveness depend on public approval and cooperation. The core conclusion is that while the principles are enduring ideals, their practical application in contemporary, diverse societies is complex and continuously contested. Critics argue that the "Peelian Principles," as commonly presented, were likely invented by mid-20th-century textbooks rather than a single, codified document from 1829. The main issue is a gap between the guiding ideals and historical/contemporary police practices, which have often shown partiality and alignment with state power structures. The principles are often considered too general or vague to provide concrete regulatory guidance for complex modern challenges such as transnational crime, technological advancements, and a pluralized security landscape. Concepts like "the police are the public" can be seen as an ideological mystification that obscures actual power dynamics and potential for discrimination. Historical and modern policing have often struggled with the principle of impartial service, with evidence of preferential treatment for the elite, as well as targeting of minority and working-class communities. The rise of social media and citizen journalism has highlighted police use of force, leading to intense scrutiny and the potential for a significant downturn in public trust, even when force is legally justified. This challenges the Peelian ideal of using force only as a last resort when persuasion has failed.

Future Direction and Way Forward

The enduring value of the Peelian principles lies in their use as a "regulative ideal" to guide aspirations for better policing. The way forward involves: Scholars advocate for recasting the principles into more specific, legally and institutionally embedded standards that can be actively used for regulation and accountability in modern contexts. Future policing should continue to emphasize procedural justice—treating all citizens with dignity and respect, being unbiased, and allowing people to voice their concerns—as research consistently shows this builds police legitimacy and public cooperation. Policing needs to adapt to contemporary challenges, including addressing systemic inequalities, navigating the complexities of social media, and operating within a human rights framework. Ensuring police remain independent of political whims while remaining accountable to the public they serve, potentially through improved oversight mechanisms and community engagement strategies, is a critical ongoing effort. "Policing by consent" is fragile and requires continuous effort to maintain, especially among historically disenfranchised communities.

Chapter 3 | PROBLEM-ORIENTED POLICING

Herman Goldstein

Herman Goldstein passed away on January 24, 2020. The Center for Problem-Oriented Policing is a reflection of his life's work, and we will honor his legacy by continuing to advance his vision for the police in a free, open and democratic society. The late Herman Goldstein (1931-2020) was a professor emeritus at the University of Wisconsin-Madison Law School and the original architect of the problem-oriented approach to policing. His first experiences in working with the police were in Philadelphia as a graduate student in governmental administration at the University of Pennsylvania and subsequently as an assistant to the city manager of Portland, Maine. He spent two years observing on-the-street police operations in Wisconsin and Michigan as a researcher with the American Bar Foundation's Survey of the Administration of Criminal Justice, and then participated in the analysis phase of that landmark project. From 1960 to 1964, he was executive assistant to the superintendent of the Chicago Police Department, O.W. Wilson, the widely recognized architect of the professional model of policing. Professor Goldstein has published widely on problem-oriented policing, the police function, police discretion, the political accountability of the police, and the control of police misconduct.

He was co-author of *the American Bar Association Standards Relating to the Urban Police Function.* His 1977 book, *Policing a Free Society*, is among the most frequently cited works on the police. He first described the problem-oriented approach to policing in a 1979 article, which he expanded upon in his 1990 book, *Problem-Oriented Policing.* Professor Goldstein's research and writings have inspired many efforts to implement and advance problem-oriented policing in police agencies around the world. Herman's career goes back to the foundations of modern police reform. In the late 1950s, he was a staff investigator for the American Bar Foundation's 10-year study of criminal justice, where he began riding with and observing police officers. It led to the earliest-known reflections on the nature of police discretion, a seminal finding that continues to influence policing today. In the 1960s, he worked on the President's Commission on Law Enforcement and the Administration of Justice, and in the 1970s, the New York City Knapp Commission on Police Corruption.

Thirty years after the publication of Herman's *Problem-Oriented Policing*, and in spite of the persistent crashing of one trend-wave after another, the POP model still floats atop the ocean of police reform movements. There is simply nothing quite like it, and I'm stunned when I teach police academy instructors, field training officers, or police leaders, and they know very little about POP. Shame on them! For goodness's sake, get a little Goldstein in your life and wake up. Problem-Oriented Policing is such a place. Herman Goldstein was the thought-leader who created it. It is now up to courageous leaders to make problem-oriented policing a reality beyond the piecemeal lip service we see today, hidden behind armored personnel carriers, night-vision goggles, and predictive algorithms.

Introduction

According to Herman Goldstein, traditional policing is incident-driven, meaning it primarily focuses on reacting to calls for service as they occur rather than proactively addressing the underlying causes of crime. This contrasts with his proposed alternative, problem-oriented policing, which aims to analyze and solve recurring community problems. Police respond to and manage individual incidents after they happen, such as responding to a 911 call. This approach is reactive in nature, with officers dealing with problems as they arise, rather than taking preventive measures. Goldstein argued that this model is insufficient and advocated a more proactive approach in which police analyze the root causes of recurring problems to develop more effective, tailored solutions.

Herman Goldstein, a key figure in community policing thought, introduced the concept of Problem-Oriented Policing (POP) as a strategic approach to address the root causes of crime rather than merely responding to individual incidents [1]. Goldstein argued that the effectiveness of traditional, incident-driven policing was limited and that police forces needed to proactively identify and solve persistent community problems [1]. The core of his framework is the SARA model, a cyclical problem-solving methodology:

Scanning: Identifying and prioritizing recurring community problems [1].

Analysis: Deeply examining the underlying causes and contributing factors of the identified problem, utilizing data from various sources [1].

Response: Developing and implementing tailored solutions designed to address the specific causes identified during the analysis phase [1].

Assessment: Evaluating the impact and effectiveness of the responses to determine if the problem has been solved or reduced, allowing for adjustments as needed [1].

POP is a foundational element of modern community policing philosophy, shifting the focus toward long-term, community-centered solutions and systemic improvements in public safety [1]. It focuses on the development of POP, moving beyond incident-driven policing to addressing underlying causes of crime using the SARA model (Scanning, Analysis, Response, and

Assessment). Herman Goldstein developed problem-oriented policing (POP) to focus police on proactively addressing chronic problems rather than relying on traditional reactive efforts.

Key Objectives

The core objectives of the study and practice of Problem-Oriented Policing (POP), as developed by Herman Goldstein, are to move police work beyond a reactive, incident-driven approach toward a proactive method focused on identifying, analyzing, and developing tailored, long-term solutions to underlying community problems that cause crime and disorder.

Shifting focus from "means" to "ends": To redirect police attention from the efficiency of internal processes (e.g., response times, number of arrests) to the actual goal or "end" of policing: reducing crime, disorder, and enhancing community safety.

Ends (Goals)

The "means versus ends" debate in policing asks whether the police's ethical goals (ends) justify potentially problematic methods (means). Effectiveness can be judged by both, with ends focusing on achieving goals like public safety, while means evaluating the methods used, such as the use of force, deception, or invasion of privacy, which are often debated in terms of their ethical justification. A focus on means is often seen as more aligned with democratic principles and as a way to uphold public trust. The outcomes and objectives of policing include reducing crime rates, maintaining public order, and ensuring public safety.

Example: Successfully apprehending a dangerous criminal to prevent future harm.

Measurement: Measured through statistics like crime resolution rates, conviction rates, and reduction in specific types of crime.

Means (Methods)

The actions and techniques police use to achieve their goals, which can include force, deception, and invasions of privacy.

Example: Using undercover operations, using force to detain a suspect, or conducting a search. The debate is whether these methods are justifiable, even if they lead to a positive outcome.

"Ends Justify the Means": This common argument suggests that if the ultimate goal is a good one (e.g., catching a terrorist), then any method used to get there is acceptable. It focuses on the rightness of the action itself, regardless of the outcome. This approach emphasizes that certain actions are inherently wrong, even for a good cause. It focuses on the consequences of an action, weighing the good outcomes against the bad ones to find the best result for the greatest number of people. Over-emphasizing ends can lead to "noble cause corruption," in which officers believe their "good" intentions justify breaking rules, thereby eroding public trust.

The solution: Police training and organizational structures should encourage officers to use ethical means and apply discretion thoughtfully, rather than as a license to ignore rules.

Key Thinkers and Concepts

The community policing philosophy and, more specifically, the strategy of **problem-oriented policing (POP)**, championed by thinkers like **Herman Goldstein**, advocate for addressing root causes, developing tailor-made responses, and expanding partnerships to improve public safety.

Herman Goldstein

In 1979, Professor Herman Goldstein proposed that police shift their focus from reactive policing—responding to crime by arresting people committing it—to a proactive approach, identifying the causes of crime, taking steps to minimize or eliminate these agents, and working with community members to develop solutions. Problem-oriented policing (POP) is a proactive crime reduction strategy that identifies and addresses the root causes of crime, unlike traditional reactive policing. Coined by Herman Goldstein in the 1970s, it uses a systematic process. Often, the SARA model, Goldstein's work over five decades, covered the most important aspects of policing in democratic societies: the broad nature of the police function, political accountability of the police, the exercise and control of police discretion, the control of police misconduct, and the many dimensions of police administration.

Key Components of POP

- Preventing crime by addressing underlying causes rather than just reacting to criminal incidents.
- Treating specific problems (such as recurring thefts in one area) as the fundamental unit of police work rather than individual crimes.
- Working with the community and other public and private organizations to develop solutions.
- Using a structured approach, commonly the SARA model, to guide the problem-solving process:
  - ✓ **Scanning:** Identifying and defining the problem.
  - ✓ **Analysis:** Investigating the causes and characteristics of the problem.
  - ✓ **Response:** Implementing solutions tailored to the analysis.
  - ✓ **Assessment:** Evaluating the effectiveness of the response.

A police department might identify that many drug crimes are happening near abandoned properties. Using POP, they would analyze why this is happening and then work with the community and city officials to have the properties boarded up or torn down, addressing the root condition. Studies show POP is effective at reducing crime and disorder, although its effects on police legitimacy and fear of crime can be limited. Evaluating POP can be complex, as measuring preventive outcomes is challenging. There is also a risk of overreach, corruption, or abuse of authority when officers intervene before a crime has actually occurred.

The Objectives of Pop

- To encourage police to systematically examine the underlying conditions, causes, and factors that contribute to specific problems, rather than just reacting to the symptoms (individual calls for service).
- To move away from a limited set of standard law enforcement tools (such as arrest or patrol) and encourage the development of creative, tailor-made interventions that directly address the specific problem at hand.
- To broaden the range of issues police address beyond just serious crime to include social and physical disorder, and
- To engage a wide array of partners (other government agencies, community organizations, private sector, and citizens) in sharing responsibility for public safety problems.
- To institutionalize a structured, iterative process for addressing problems, commonly operationalized through the SARA model:
  - ✓ Identifying and prioritizing recurring problems.
  - ✓ Deeply researching the problem, victims, offenders, and the context (why they all come together at a specific time and place).
  - ✓ Implementing creative solutions that extend beyond traditional policing methods.
  - ✓ Evaluating the effectiveness of the responses and making adjustments as needed.

Ultimately, the objective is to make policing more effective at reducing crime and disorder in the long term, while doing so in a cost-effective manner.

The approach seeks long-lasting solutions rather than temporary fixes.

Partnership

Examples of problem-oriented policing partnerships include Chicago's strategy for addressing drug sales, which involves collaborating with community members to identify specific problem areas and develop targeted, long-term solutions. Other examples include partnerships with social service agencies, schools, and community organizations to address the root causes of crime, such as homelessness, mental health issues, or a lack of youth programs.

Chicago's Drug and Gang Initiative

The city identified a two- to three-block area with a high number of drug complaints and implemented a multifaceted strategy that included working with the community to identify problem areas rather than just responding to calls.

- **Community and Social Service Collaboration:** Police departments partner with social service agencies to address underlying issues that contribute to crime, such as providing mental health support, substance abuse treatment, or housing assistance to individuals who repeatedly come into contact with law enforcement.

School-based Partnerships

Law enforcement works with schools to create programs that address truancy, bullying, or youth violence by engaging with students, parents, and teachers to develop preventive strategies and educational initiatives.

Businessand Community Partnerships

Police work with business owners to address specific problems, such as shoplifting or loitering, by developing solutions together, including improving lighting, increasing security, or establishing communication between businesses and the police.

John Eck and William Spelman

John Eck and William Spelman developed the SARA model, an acronym for the four-step problem-solving process of Scanning, Analysis, Response, and Assessment, to guide problem-oriented policing. It involves identifying problems (Scanning), thoroughly investigating their causes (Analysis), implementing a solution (Response), and evaluating the outcome (Assessment). The model was developed in collaboration with the Newport News Police Department and is a cornerstone of problem-oriented policing.

The Four Steps of the SARA Model

- **Scanning:** Identifying and prioritizing potential problems in a community that may contribute to crime and disorder.
- **Analysis:** Collecting and analyzing data about the identified problem to understand its nature, scope, and underlying causes.
- **Response:** Developing and implementing interventions designed to solve or reduce the problem. This can involve other agencies and community members.
- **Assessment:** Evaluating the effectiveness of the response and using the results to refine the solution or address any new problems that may have arisen.

George Kelling and James Q. Wilson

Their "Broken Windows" theory (1982) contributed to the community policing movement by suggesting that addressing minor signs of social and physical disorder (e.g., broken windows, graffiti) can prevent more serious crime from taking root, aligning with the expanded mandate to address quality-of-life issues. The thinkers and models mentioned are central to the following principles described in your request: Goldstein, Eck, and Spelman emphasized that police should move beyond reactive, incident-driven policing to systematically examine the underlying factors (situational opportunities, social issues, physical environment) that contribute to problems.

The SARA model, central to POP, explicitly calls for a broad, "uninhibited" search for appropriate, customized responses rather than relying solely on arrests or patrol. These thinkers advocated for a broader police role that includes addressing social and physical disorder and engaging with a wide array of partners, including other government agencies, community organizations, and private citizens, to share responsibility for public safety.

Problem-Oriented Policing

POP is an effective strategy for reducing crime by proactively addressing the underlying causes of community problems, thereby shifting from traditional reactive policing. Subsequent evidence supports POP's effectiveness, showing statistically significant reductions in crime and disorder where it has been implemented, although challenges to full implementation still exist.

Conclusion

An "end of part-1 conclusion" is a summary and final thought for a section of work that restates the main points, connects them back to the overall thesis or question, and leaves the reader with a sense of closure and final understanding. It is crucial to avoid introducing new information or arguments and instead focus on synthesizing the ideas already presented, providing a final analysis of their significance. The core conclusion is that community policing is a fundamental philosophy and organizational strategy based on the idea that police and citizens must become partners to effectively address the root causes of crime and disorder. Its success is rooted in building trust, fostering collaboration, and shifting from a reactive "us versus them" mentality to a proactive, shared responsibility for public safety. The philosophical foundation of community policing can be traced back to the principles of Sir Robert Peel in 1829, which held that "a policeman is a citizen with a uniform and a citizen is a policeman without a uniform," emphasizing that policing is by consent and requires public support. Several key thinkers contributed significantly to the development of the philosophy of community policing:

Sir Robert Peel
Often considered the "father of modern policing," his 1829 Peelian Principles emphasized that "the basic mission for which the police exist is to prevent crime and disorder" and that "the ability of the police to perform their duties is dependent upon public approval". This established the core idea of "policing by consent," which is central to community policing today.

Herman Goldstein
In 1979, Goldstein introduced the concept of Problem-Oriented Policing (POP), arguing that the police should move beyond simply responding to individual incidents and instead identify and address the underlying causes of recurring problems in the community.

James Q. Wilson and George Kelling
Their influential 1982 "Broken Windows" theory suggested that visible signs of social disorder (like a broken window left unrepaired) create an environment that encourages more serious crime. They advocated for swift community-based intervention to address minor issues as a means of preventing urban decay and escalating crime.

Robert Trojanowicz and Bonnie Bucqueroux
Their work provided a practical framework for community policing, emphasizing elements such as community empowerment, shared responsibility, and the police officer's role as a direct link to the neighborhood.

Robert Friedmann
In 1992, Friedmann offered a comprehensive definition of community policing as a "policy and a strategy aimed at achieving

more effective and efficient crime control, reduced fear of crime, improved quality of life through a proactive reliance on community resources that seeks to change crime-causing conditions."

Conclusion of the Philosophy

In conclusion, the foundation of the community policing philosophy is built upon these core tenets. The police and citizens are equal partners in identifying, prioritizing, and solving problems, thereby building trust and cooperation. The focus is on proactively addressing the root causes of crime and disorder using systematic methods, such as the SARA model (Scanning, Analysis, Response, Assessment), rather than just reacting to calls for service. The ultimate goal is crime prevention and the enhancement of the overall quality of life and sense of security within the community. It requires internal organizational change, including decentralizing authority and granting officers more autonomy to make decisions at the local level, while also increasing police accountability to the public. This philosophy represents a significant departure from the traditional, isolated, and solely law-enforcement-focused model, aiming instead for a collaborative, holistic, and democratic approach to public safety. Key theoretical foundations and principles include:

- Developing collaborative relationships with community members, local government agencies, non-profits, and private businesses to identify and solve problems, realigning police agency management, structure, and personnel to support community engagement and decentralized decision-making, often requiring a shift in police culture.
- Proactively addressing the underlying conditions that cause crime and social disorder, rather than merely reacting to isolated incidents.

  This often involves data collection and interagency cooperation for long-term solutions (Problem-Oriented Policing).

- Emphasizing fairness, respect, and transparency in police interactions to build legitimacy and encourage public cooperation.

Thinkers' Suggestions

Leading thinkers and scholars have offered key suggestions for effective implementation. Robert Trojanowicz and Bonnie Bucqueroux focused on practical implementation, stressing the need for officers to be permanently stationed in specific areas (e.g., foot patrols) to build strong neighborhood relationships. George Kelling and James Q. Wilson are associated with the "Broken Windows" theory, which, while debated, influenced community policing by highlighting the importance of addressing visible signs of disorder to deter more serious crime and fear of crime. David Bayley and other critics have raised concerns that community policing might lead to a reduction in crime-control effectiveness or to the imposition of "particularistic community normative standards" that can raise civil rights issues. They suggest a balanced approach is needed. Modern researchers suggest that police leadership must genuinely support the philosophy and provide clear guidance to frontline officers, moving beyond a "rhetoric" of community policing to sincere, daily proactive engagement.

Future Direction

The future of community policing involves several key directions:

- Utilizing e-community policing platforms, data analytics, and communication tools to enhance accessibility, transparency, and information sharing between the police and the public.
- A greater emphasis on addressing social issues that fuel crime (such as poverty and substance abuse) through cross-agency collaboration (e.g., involving social services, healthcare providers, and schools).

  The approach is increasingly recognized as the philosophical foundation for democratic policing, demanding greater accountability, respect for human rights, and transparency in police operations.

- Evolving to address contemporary concerns such as homeland security and cybercrime while maintaining core community engagement principles to prevent social divisions.

In conclusion, community policing continues to be viewed as a vital, long-term strategic approach for enhancing public safety and quality of life through mutual trust and collaboration between law enforcement and the diverse communities they serve.

Part II
Key Thinkers and Core Theories

Introduction

Key thinkers in community policing theory include Sir Robert Peel, Herman Goldstein, James Q. Wilson, and George Kelling. Their ideas established foundational principles like "policing by consent," problem-solving, and addressing disorder to prevent serious crime.

Sir Robert Peel: Although living in the 19th century, his principles for the London Metropolitan Police are considered the philosophical foundation for modern democratic policing and community policing. His core idea was "policing by consent," emphasizing that the police's power depends on public approval and cooperation rather than force.

Herman Goldstein: A US sociologist, Goldstein argued that police had become too procedure-focused and needed to tackle the root causes of crime in collaboration with the community. He developed the concept of Problem-Oriented Policing (POP), a structured approach in which officers proactively identify and solve the underlying issues that generate repeated calls for service, rather than just reacting to incidents.

James Q. Wilson and George Kelling: Their influential 1982 article, "Broken Windows: The Police and Neighborhood Safety," introduced the Broken Windows Theory. This theory suggests that visible signs of physical and social disorder (like broken windows, graffiti, and loitering) create an environment that encourages further, more serious crime. Their work advocates a proactive police role in addressing minor offences and disorder to maintain social order and prevent neighborhood decay, often in collaboration with the community.

Robert Trojanowicz and Bonnie Bucqueroux: These researchers were instrumental in defining the philosophy of community policing in the late 20th century, describing it as a partnership between the public and the police to address public safety challenges and improve overall quality of life. The philosophy of community policing is underpinned by several core theories:

- **Policing by Consent:** This foundational principle from Peel asserts that the legitimacy and effectiveness of the police depend on the public's approval and willingness to cooperate with them.
- **Problem-Oriented Policing (POP):** A central strategy focusing on identifying and analyzing the underlying causes of recurring crime and disorder problems and developing tailored solutions, rather than just responding to individual incidents.
- **Broken Windows Theory:** This theory posits that maintaining order and addressing minor signs of decay can prevent the escalation to serious crime by creating an environment where criminal activity is less likely to thrive.
- **Communitarian Theory:** This theory argues that communities have a shared responsibility to participate in fighting crime and maintaining informal social control, moving away from relying solely on the police as the primary agency for social control.
- **Normative Sponsorship Theory:** This highlights the importance of trust and collaboration between law enforcement and the community, emphasizing the need for strong relationships to effectively address local issues.

Chapter 4 | THE "BROKEN WINDOWS" THEORY

James Q. Wilson

James Q. Wilson, an influential political scientist who was a leading theorist on crime, morality and families, and who was the co-author of the influential "broken-windows" theory, which led to community policing efforts throughout the country, died March 2 at a hospital in Boston. He was 80. BOSTON (AP) — Political scientist James Q. Wilson, whose "broken windows" theory on crime-fighting emphasized attacking small problems to prevent bigger ones and helped trigger a nationwide move toward community policing, died Friday at a Boston hospital. He was 80. Wilson wrote or co-authored more than a dozen books on various topics, but his study of police work has resonated for decades. He was a distinguished scholar in Boston College's political science department at the time of his death. The ideas in his 1982 "Broken Windows" article in *The Atlantic* influenced successful community policing efforts in cities including New York and Los Angeles. Last month, Detroit announced it was beginning its own initiative. "He's just clearly one of the foremost social scientists of the second half of the 20th century," Skerry said. "He was a very on-the-ground kind of scholar and brought a great insight and common sense to things."

Wilson and co-author George L. Kelling argued in *The Atlantic* article that communities must address minor crimes and their effects, such as broken windows, to prevent larger problems from developing. "I think Jim and I caught a wind," Kelling said in an interview on Friday. "Up until that time in policing, nothing seemed to work. By the late 70s, policing was kind of looking for a new approach and community policing was kind of on the horizon, although not yet being really articulated." Kelling said the article instantly resonated with law enforcement, who knew it was true from experience, but it also caught the general public's attention because the "broken windows" metaphor was so effective. "That was pure Wilson," said Kelling, now a fellow at the Manhattan Institute for Policy Research. "The thing about a metaphor is it takes a complex thing and simplifies it and makes it readily graspable." The article was based on firsthand research — Kelling walked the beat alongside Newark, N.J., police during the 1970s — as well as the work of other scientists. In it, Wilson and Kelling argued that policing had historically been about maintaining order, but had become overly focused on solving serious crimes.

Introduction

In 1982, George L. Kelling and James Q. Wilson introduced their famous broken windows theory, which explains the emergence of serious crime through disorder in the community. According to it, local disorders such as profanity, public intoxication, litter, graffiti and residents' apathy create ideal circumstances for an increase in serious violent crimes. (Kelling & Wilson, as cited in Jefferson, 2016). In other words, if residents cannot maintain the positive appearance of their neighborhood in relatively minor matters, their community is likely to descend into a downward spiral of severe crime. The disorder leads to fear; fear creates disengagement and a sense of apathy, which in turn results in a surge of crime. The rising crime rates and overall decline eventually lead to a mass exodus from the community, as everyone who can do so tries to flee from the depressing environment (Konkel et al., 2019). The theory became popular among law enforcers and policymakers, who attempted to utilize it in practice in troubled communities.

New York City was one of the pioneers in the broad implementation of the broken windows theory. In 1994, New York's mayor, Rudolph Giuliani, and the NYPD initiated a police reform that shifted the department's focus from serious crimes to local disorder in problematic areas (Kelling and Bratton, as cited in Jefferson, 2016). Police Strategy No.5 targeted "lower grade offences" and symbols of disorder such as beggars, loiterers, visibly mentally ill persons, sex workers, and graffiti writers (Jefferson, 2016). Mayor Michael Bloomberg expanded this campaign even further: operations "Clean Sweep" (2002), "Spotlight" (2002), "Impact" (2003) and "High Housing" (2004) targeted public alcohol and marijuana users and deployed extra police officers (Jefferson, 2016). The broken windows theory served as a prominent framework for all these actions. In theory, addressing the local issues would have improved New York's appearance and positively affect the criminal justice system by reducing the number of serious crimes. Nowadays, the broken windows theory is being criticized on multiple levels. For example, Kamalu and Onyeozili (2018) argue that broken windows policing has significant negative implications on a societal level. Firstly, it diverts significant resources from social programs like drug treatment and education to incarcerations and jail maintenance. In other words, strict law enforcement aggressively treats symptoms rather than the problem itself. Secondly, its uncompromising approach to minor offences leads to general hostility towards the police and undermines public policing legitimacy. As a result, community residents begin to see police officers as enemies rather than protectors against crime (Kamalu & Onyeozili, 2018). In some instances, community members from ethnic minorities can even characterize the broken windows approach to criminal justice as "racialized rudeness, rough treatment and abuse" (Fisher, as cited in Jefferson, 2016). Therefore, the purpose of this essay lies in evaluating the effectiveness of broken windows theory and its implications on the criminal justice system at the community level.

During the 1970s, twenty-eight cities in New Jersey took part in a pilot project known as the Safe and Clean Neighborhoods Program. The program delivered funding to cities that allowed police departments to establish more foot patrols, thereby increasing the visible presence of law enforcement officers on local streets. These foot patrol officers took a no-tolerance stance on low-level crime while working to establish unwritten rules of proper conduct and gain the trust and goodwill of community members. After five years, the Police Foundation in Washington DC released the results of a review that measured the effectiveness of the program. That review found that while actual crime rates had not been significantly reduced, local residents reported that they felt safer because of the increased police presence in their neighborhoods. It also reported that residents living in areas where the foot patrols were conducted had more positive opinions of the police. Similarly, police officers working foot patrol beats reported a stronger sense of connection to the local community and higher levels of career satisfaction, compared to officers assigned to squad car duty.

This pilot project formed the basis of Wilson and Kelling's broken windows theory, which was first explained in an article titled "Broken Windows: The Police and Neighborhood Safety," published in *the Atlantic* magazine in March of 1982. Kelling, who had routinely accompanied police officers during foot patrols in Newark, New Jersey, was also one of the authors of the Police Foundation review of the project. According to Kelling's view, the initial program's statistical effect on crime may have been minimal, but its psychological effect on both local residents and those who commit crimes was immense. Together with Wilson, Kelling developed a theory based on his experiences. It essentially forwarded the idea that using unofficial but clearly understood rules to establish order in a problem area encouraged locals to stay within the bounds of acceptable conduct. Coming to be known as the broken windows theory, the idea was further developed by additional theorists and came to include two major hypotheses. The first hypothesis is that a prevailing sense of order in a neighborhood reduces low-level criminal activity. Second, this reduction in low-level criminal activity prevents more serious crime from ever taking place.

The "Broken Windows" theory, introduced by criminologists James Q. Wilson and George Kelling in a 1982 article for *The Atlantic*, suggests that visible signs of physical and social disorder in a neighborhood can encourage more serious crime. The core idea is that a single broken window left unrepaired signals a lack of care and control, which in turn leads to a breakdown of community standards and informal social controls. This perception of apathy or disorder can make residents feel less safe and more likely to withdraw from public life, thus creating an environment where criminal behavior is more likely to occur and escalate. The theory advocates "order-maintenance" policing strategies that focus on addressing minor offences such as vandalism, loitering, and public drunkenness to prevent the "spiral of decay" from taking hold. The goal of this approach is not only to deter serious crime but also to improve community safety perceptions and restore a sense of lawfulness and order. It discusses how physical disorder leads to social disorder and serious crime, the role of maintenance, and the impact on community safety perceptions. The core objective of community policing, as envisioned by its key thinkers and underlying theories, is to make communities safer and more secure by fostering collaboration and trust between law enforcement and the public, moving beyond traditional enforcement methods. While community policing is a broad philosophy, several key thinkers and the theories they proposed or utilized shaped its objectives:

The Broken Windows theory, proposed by George L. Kelling and James Q. Wilson in a 1982 article, suggests that visible signs of disorder like broken windows, graffiti, and litter can lead to a decline in social respect, which in turn encourages more serious crime. The theory argues that addressing minor disorders, such as stricter policing of minor offences, can help prevent more serious crimes by signaling that a community respects order. The theory posits a causal link between disorder and crime. Visible signs of neglect, like a broken window, signal that no one cares about the property or the community. This perception of indifference emboldens criminals, leading to more serious crimes. The theory's proponents suggest that policing should focus on maintaining order by cracking down on minor crimes, like vandalism, public drinking, and loitering. The theory was popularized in the 1990s by New York City Police Commissioner William Bratton, who influenced policing policies that focused on minor offenses, such as fare evasion and public urination.

Criticism: The theory has been controversial, with critics questioning its effectiveness and the fairness of its application, particularly in relation to practices such as "stop-and-frisk".

Herman Goldstein (Problem-Oriented Policing)

Herman Goldstein advocated for a shift from a reactive, incident-driven police model to one that actively identifies and addresses underlying community problems that cause crime and disorder. The objective is to develop effective, long-term solutions to specific, recurring issues rather than just responding to individual calls. The SARA (Scanning, Analysis, Response, and Assessment) model is a direct application of this approach. Herman Goldstein developed the concept of Problem-Oriented Policing (POP), a strategy that focuses on identifying and addressing the root causes of crime rather than just responding to incidents. The SARA model (Scanning, Analysis, Response, and Assessment) was later developed by Eck and Spelman to provide a structured framework for implementing Goldstein's POP strategy.

Problem-Oriented Policing (POP)

Instead of the traditional reactive model, POP is a proactive approach that involves police departments identifying and analyzing chronic problems that contribute to crime and disorder, and developing and implementing specific solutions to prevent their recurrence. This often involves working with the community and private organizations to address underlying issues, such as drug sales, gang activity, or traffic hazards.

SARAModel

The SARA model is a four-step process used to execute POP:

- Scanning: Identify and define specific, recurring problems in the community. This involves sorting out problems and gathering initial details about who, what, when, and where.
- Analysis: Conduct an in-depth study of the problem to understand its causes and contributing factors. This step seeks to answer the "why" behind the problem, using various analytical methods such as trend or pattern analysis.
- Response: Develop and implement solutions tailored to the specific problem identified during the analysis phase. This can involve a variety of innovative approaches.
- Assessment: Evaluate the effectiveness of the implemented response to see if the problem has been addressed. If not, the process can be adjusted and repeated.

The broken windows theory suggests that visible signs of crime, anti-social behavior and social disorder can create an environment which fosters more serious crimes. These visible signs of crime can include vandalism, graffiti, littering, fly tipping and neglected or damaged property, such as broken windows, which is where the theory found its name.

The theory states that visible signs of crime and neglect indicate that no one in a community cares. This perception leads to more crime, with an escalating level of severity and can leave people feeling an area is no longer safe. The Broken Windows theory was introduced by George L. Kelling and James Q. Wilson in an article in *The Atlantic* in 1982. The article included criticism of how the police handled certain crimes – such as those outlined above – and suggested that this mishandling would have a detrimental effect on communities. They argued that better policing of minor disorder would help maintain public order and prevent more serious crime, stating that the theory is named after an analogy used to explain it. If a window in a building is broken and remains unrepaired for too long, the rest of the windows in that building will eventually be broken, too. According to Wilson and Kelling, this is because the unrepaired window signals to people in that neighborhood that they can break windows without fear of consequences, since nobody cares enough to stop it or fix it. Eventually, Wilson and Kelling argued that more serious crimes like robbery and violence would flourish. The idea is that physical signs of neglect and deterioration encourage criminal behavior because they act as a signal that this is a place where disorder is allowed to persist. If no one cares enough to pick up the litter on the sidewalk or repair and reuse abandoned buildings, maybe they will not care enough to call the police when they see a drug deal or a burglary either.

The theory sparked a wave of "broken windows" or "zero tolerance" policing, where law enforcement began cracking down on non-violent behaviors like loitering, graffiti, or panhandling. By ramping up arrests and citations for perceived disorderly behavior and removing physical signs of disorder from the neighborhood, police hope to create a more orderly environment that discourages more serious crime. The broken windows theory has been used beyond policing, including in the workplace and schools. Using a similar zero-tolerance approach that disciplines students or employees for minor violations is thought to create more orderly environments that foster learning and productivity.

"By discouraging small acts of misconduct, such as tardiness, minor rule violations, or unprofessional conduct, employers seek to promote a culture of accountability, professionalism, and high performance," said David Tzall, Psy.D., a licensed forensic psychologist and Deputy Director for the Health and Wellness Unit of the NYPD. While the idea that one broken window leads to many sounds plausible, subsequent research failed to find a connection. "The theory oversimplifies the causes of crime by focusing primarily on visible signs of disorder," Tzall said. "It neglects underlying social and economic factors, such as poverty, unemployment, and lack of education, which are known to be important contributors to criminal behavior." When researchers account for those underlying factors, the connection between disordered environments and crime rates disappears.

In a 2016 report,3 the NYPD found that its "quality-of-life" policing—another term for broken windows policing—had no impact on the city's crime rate. Between 2010 and 2015, the number of "quality-of-life" summons issued by the NYPD for offences such as open containers, public urination, and riding bicycles on the sidewalk dropped by about 33%. While the broken windows theory would theorize that serious crimes would spike when the police stopped cracking down on those minor offenses, violent crimes and property crimes actually decreased during that same time period. "Policing based on broken windows theory has never been shown to work," said Kimberly Vered Shashoua, LCSW, a therapist who works with marginalized teens and young adults. Criminalizing unhoused people, low socio-economic status households, and others who create this type of 'crime' does not get to the root of the problem. Not only have policing efforts that focus on things like graffiti or panhandling failed to have any impact on violent crime, but they have often been used to target marginalized communities. The theory's implementation can lead to biased policing practices as law enforcement officers can concentrate their efforts on low-income neighborhoods or communities predominantly populated by minority groups. That biased policing happens, in part, because there is no objective measure of disordered environments so there is a lot of room for implicit bias and discrimination to influence decision-making about which neighborhoods to target in crackdowns.

Studies show that neighborhoods where residents are predominantly Black or Latino are perceived as more disorderly and prone to crime than neighborhoods where residents are mostly white, even when police-recorded crime rates and physical signs of physical deterioration in the environment were the same.

Moreover, many of the behaviors that are used by police and researchers as signs of disorder are influenced by racial and class bias. Drinking and hanging out are both legal activities that are viewed as orderly when they happen in private spaces like a home or bar, for example. But those who socialize and drink in parks or on stoops outside their building are viewed as disorderly and charged with loitering and public drunkenness.4

While the broken windows theory and its application are flawed, the underlying idea that our physical environment can influence our behavior does hold some water. On one hand, "the physical environment conveys social norms that influence our behavior," Tzall explained. "When we observe others adhering to certain norms in a particular space, we tend to adjust our own behavior to align with them."

If a person sees litter on the street, they might be more likely to litter themselves, for example. But that does not necessarily mean they will make the leap from littering to robbery or violent assault. Moreover, litter can often be a sign that there are not enough public trash cans available on the streets for people to throw away food wrappers and other waste while they are out. In that scenario, installing more trash cans would do far more to reduce litter than increasing the number of citations for littering.

"The design and layout of spaces can also signal specific expectations and guide our actions," Tzall explained. In the litter example, then, the addition of more trash cans can also act as an environmental cue to encourage throwing trash away rather than littering.

Ultimately, reducing crime requires addressing the root causes of poverty and social inequality that lead to crime. But taking care of public spaces and neighborhoods to keep them clean and enjoyable can still have a positive impact on the communities that live in and use them.

"Positive environments provide opportunities for meaningful interactions and collaboration among community members," Tzall said. Access to green spaces, recreational facilities, mental health resources, and community services contributes to physical, mental, and emotional health.

By creating more positive environments, we can encourage healthier lifestyle choices—like adding protected bike lanes to encourage people to ride bikes—and prosocial behavior—like adding basketball courts in parks to encourage people to meet and play a game with their neighbors. At the individual level, Tzall suggests people "can initiate or participate in community projects, volunteer for local organizations, support inclusive initiatives, engage in dialogue with neighbors, and collaborate with local authorities or community leaders." We can create positive environments by taking the initiative to pick up litter when we see it, participating in tree-planting initiatives, collaborating with our neighbors to establish a community garden, or volunteering with a local organization to advocate for better public spaces and resources.

Impact

The single best-known application of the broken windows theory took place in the 1990s in New York City, under the administration of Mayor Rudy Giuliani and police commissioner William Bratton. Giuliani and Bratton urged aggressive prosecution of low-level crimes, resulting in a 70 percent increase in misdemeanor arrests for relatively minor offences over the 1990s. During that time, criminal activity in New York City dropped at rates that far outpaced the nationwide average in the United States. Violent crime in New York fell by more than 56 percent, compared with 28 percent nationwide. Property crime declined by 65 percent in the city, compared with 26 percent nationwide.

Further analysis seemed to reveal an immediate, noticeable impact from the time the broken windows policing policy was introduced in New York. Using a 10 percent rise in misdemeanor arrest rates as a benchmark for identifying the point at which the theory was put into practice, the corresponding rate of robberies dropped by a reported 3.2 percent, while vehicle thefts fell by as much as 2.1 percent. Supporters of the broken windows theory have argued that these statistics provide strong evidence that the theory works in the real world.

However, critics of the policy have argued that there is no proof that the crackdown on low-level crime was the reason for the dramatic reductions in violent crime and property crime. Several other possible explanations for the results have been forwarded. First, the size of New York's police force grew by more than one-third during the 1990s, while the number of people imprisoned in the city for crimes increased by 24 percent. The second half of the decade also brought an economic boom, leading to higher employment nationwide and in New York. Between 1992 and 1999, New York's unemployment rate declined by 39 percent, and statistical analysis suggests that the improved employment outlook alone could account for most of the reductions in the city's robbery and vehicle theft rates.

The broken windows theory has also been criticized for encouraging racial profiling of minority groups, particularly in African American and Latino communities. Opponents claim that it also tends to target lower-income and otherwise disadvantaged individuals, such as the unhoused, while contributing to overcrowded prisons and costly burdens to the justice system. In the summer of 2014, a man named Eric Garner died after an interaction with New York City police in the borough of Staten Island. Garner had been accused of a minor crime involving the illegal sale of loose cigarettes and was involved in a physical altercation with a police officer that was captured on video by a bystander. Garner died after being placed in a chokehold by the officer, and despite the video evidence, no charges of misconduct were brought against the officer involved in the incident. The resulting public outcry brought the broken windows theory under intense scrutiny, prompting major policy reviews and changes to New York's law enforcement standards. A similar incident resulting in the 2015 death of Baltimore resident Freddie Gray was also linked to broken windows policing policies. In the late 2010s and

2020s, a nationwide discourse on defunding the police led to additional scrutiny and major policy shifts in many police departments across the US.

Issue Identification

The broken windows theory has brought intense controversy in local communities across the US. Racialized police violence became a theme of heated discussions on the national level, and the broken windows theory is often related to police brutality cases (Jefferson, 2016). However, it is not being replaced with less controversial law enforcement practices but is spreading to other US cities, and even other countries are adopting the American experience. According to Jefferson (2016), the broken windows approach has been replicated in Buenos Aires (Argentina), Essen (Germany), London and Glasgow (United Kingdom), Tokyo (Japan), and many other cities and communities all over the world. Moreover, in 2014, the majority of New Yorkers supported the broken windows approach to law enforcement, including 57% of Black and 64% of Hispanic respondents (Jefferson, 2016). The policy showed surprising resilience despite a steady flow of controversial cases, mass protests and civilian discontent.

Therefore, the main issue for law enforcement regarding the broken windows theory is determining its actual effectiveness and its implications for community criminal justice. A researcher needs to understand the logic of the relationships between the community and law enforcement, the defendant's psychology and patterns of thinking, and the community's perception of itself by its residents and by the police. Obviously, there must be solid arguments for widespread support of the seemingly controversial policing approach, especially if it becomes an international practice. The methods of dealing with controversial aspects within the broken windows theory framework also present interest. It is challenging to draw conclusions or offer recommendations without conducting a thorough analysis of the subject. Overall, the issue of the broken windows theory in community policing and criminal justice seems to be complex and demands an all-rounded consideration.

The broken windows theory and corresponding community policing measures were developed in the 80s and 90s, but their origins can be traced back to the early 40s. Shaw and McKay argued that the residents of visibly neglected communities may be less able to articulate the strategies of social control (as cited in Konkel et al., 2019). Such a situation led to the constant coming and going of the residents with low social and psychological investment into the community and consequent increase in offences. About 40 years later, Kelling and Wilson expanded this idea into a broken windows theory. They have provided two possible pathways of disorder-provoking criminal behavior. The first pathway, which describes a direct effect of disorder on crime, is reflected in the allegory: a broken window serves as a symbol of unchecked delinquency (O'Brien et al., 2018). The second pathway is indirect: disorder leads residents to retreat from their community's public life and eventually causes it to collapse.

Several years later, the theory attracted the attention of law enforcement and criminal justice officials in troubled communities. In 1990, William J. Bratton, the Police Commissioner of New York City, instituted it under the name of "zero-tolerance" policing (Kamalu & Onyeozili, 2018). Over the years, New York's experience was copied by other American cities under different names. For instance, Albuquerque implemented a "safe streets" program, and Lowell — a "hot spots" technique that strongly reminded New York's policing measures. The broken windows theory would spread overseas, as a study by Keizer, Lindenberg, and Steg (2008, as cited in Kamalu & Onyeozili, 2018) seemed to demonstrate a correlation between disorder and increased delinquent behavior. However, other researchers have claimed that Kelling, Wilson, and their supporters overestimated the impact of disorder and underestimated the characteristics of other neighborhoods, such as poverty, racial composition, and residential stability (Konkel et al.,

2019). The question of the broken windows theory's effectiveness and its implications for criminal justice remains hotly debated today.

Analysis

As stated in the previous sections, the question of the broken windows theory's actual effectiveness and its implications for criminal justice is up for debate. The problem is complicated and requires a multi-layered analysis for sufficient understanding. Firstly, it is necessary to gain a deeper understanding of the community's perceptions among residents and law enforcement officials. Secondly, it is important to recognize that the relationships between community residents and law enforcement officials can be viewed through the lens of criminal law. And only after completing all these steps will it be possible to assess the effectiveness of the broken windows theory and provide recommendations for policing.

The broken windows theory can be viewed as a proactive policing approach to curbing crime, as it focuses on eliminating potential causes of criminal behaviour. Therefore, it theoretically serves to increase the feeling of safety and promote the general well-being of the residents (Stein &Griffith, 2017). Ideally, police officers and residents should work together so that the policing framework reflects officers' perceptions of the community and the neighbourhood's actual needs. In practice, the residents of the neighborhoods with high crime rates are the most resistant and mistrustful of criminal justice policing because they treat the police officers as outsiders (Stein & Griffith, 2017). Data from Kamalu and Onyeozili (2018) show that more than 80% of New York City residents, who were stopped by police officers between 2002 and 2015, were innocent. Such indiscriminate law-enforcing efforts can cause hostility towards the police and hamper criminal justice policing in the community.

On the other hand, officers who follow the strict zero-tolerance guidelines of the broken windows theory might develop a distorted view of the neighborhood and overreact to minor offences. Misaligned perceptions of a community as more problematic than it is may lead to differences in views on crime prevention between the police and residents (Stein & Griffith, 2017). In theory, it can even lead to situations in which covering up a minor offence is preferable to calling the police. The residents would be too scared to call the police and would choose not to interfere, or, in the worst-case scenario, would try to serve justice themselves.

Criminal law has various functions, and crime prevention or punishment for criminal offences is among the most notable. In the broken windows theory, one might see a shift in behavioral and socioeconomic concepts into a category within criminal law. Community policing, based on the theory, seeks to eliminate disorder and minor offences to prevent the surge of serious crimes. There is nothing wrong with seeing criminal law as a punitive institution; however, it would be wrong to limit criminal law to punishment alone (Simester, 2021). In that regard, community policing based on the broken windows theory steps into dangerous territory, since it relies on punishing those responsible for disorder above all else.

Such an approach can be harmful to the image of law enforcement bodies and community policing efforts alike. The wrongdoing principle in criminal law requires identifying the legally prohibited wrong that the defendant actually did (Simester, 2021). From the broken windows theory's perspective, people contributing to the disorder are morally wrong since they disrupt the community's life. Therefore, preemptive actions against them, such as arrests on the streets or incarcerations, are justified. However, residents of troubled communities often have a different perspective that law enforcers do not consider. Community residents can even consider certain behavior normative or non-threatening (Harcourt, as cited in Konkel et al., 2019). As a result, the residents become mistrustful, the officers resort to unnecessarily harsh actions, and the animosity between the police and the neighborhood's population grows.

The biggest irony of the broken windows theory is that it is based on a correlation drawn from a single experiment. Kelling and

Wilson founded their theory on Zimbardo's car experiment, in which a car abandoned in a poor, predominantly black neighborhood was quickly stripped for spare parts (Konkel et al., 2019). On the contrary, the car left in a standard neighborhood with mostly white residents did not attract attention until the researchers deliberately damaged it. Quite obviously, that disorder in the neighborhood could not be the only reason for such different outcomes. Moreover, it may have had little relevance, and the residents' living standards may have been a more important factor.

Therefore, the broken windows theory can be considered a behavioral hypothesis with an implied outcome rather than a solid pattern. Regarding the criminal justice system, it seems to have quite dangerous implications since it diverts the time and resources of police officers and causes animosity between them and the community residents. Broken windows community policing puts extreme pressure on officers and forces them to take punitive actions, which often worsen their public image and breed mutual mistrust. To mitigate these issues, police departments can shift their focus to curbing serious crime, engage residents in community policing, and implement multicultural awareness programs for officers. After all, the broken windows theory is not harmful per se; it is better suited for matters outside the criminal justice field.

Criticism and Limitations

While the Broken Windows Theory has its merits, it is not without its critics, who argue that it confuses correlation with causation. A decline in crime rates may not necessarily result from addressing minor disorder. Strict enforcement of minor offenses can disproportionately target marginalized communities, leading to social tensions and perceptions of unfair treatment. The effectiveness of the theory may vary depending on cultural, economic, and social contexts. What works in one city might not apply in another.

Concept Description Key Difference

The Broken Windows Theory focuses on addressing minor disorder to prevent serious crime and emphasizes the physical and social signs of disorder.

Routine Activity Theory suggests that crime occurs when a motivated offender, a suitable target, and a lack of guardianship converge, and it focuses on situational factors rather than environmental signals.

Social Disorganization Theory attributes crime to the breakdown of social structures and community ties in neighborhoods and focuses on community dynamics rather than visible signs of neglect.

Crime Prevention through Environmental Design (CPTED) advocates designing physical spaces to reduce opportunities for crime and emphasizes proactive design and architecture rather than reactive responses to disorder.

Conclusion

The Broken Windows Theory underscores the importance of maintaining order to foster a sense of safety and prevent crime. While its applications have led to positive outcomes in some cases, it is essential to approach the theory critically and adapt its principles to diverse contexts. By balancing enforcement with community engagement and fairness, societies can work toward safer, more inclusive environments. Read More: https://polilegal.com/post/understanding-the-broken-windows-theory/

Chapter 5 | BUILDING POLICE-COMMUNITY PARTNERSHIPS

Robert Trojanowicz

Robert Trojanowicz graduated from Michigan State University, earning a Bachelor of Arts degree in Police Administration in 1963, a Master of Social Work in 1965 and a PhD in Social Science with specializations in political science, police administration and sociology in 1969. Robert Trojanowicz was a professor and Director of the School of Criminal Justice for 25 years and an academic advocate of community policing.

Robert Trojanowicz was a pioneer in the community policing movement by directing cutting-edge research through the Flint (Michigan) Neighborhood Foot Patrol Program, which encouraged cooperation between the police and the community to solve local crime problems and build relationships. This "new" policing concept helped launch the community policing movement by restructuring police priorities to give entire communities the best chance of becoming safer and by helping make all neighborhoods more crime- and drug-resistant. Robert Trojanowicz later became the founder and served as Director of the National Center for Community Policing. Robert Trojanowicz was a consultant to police agencies in the United States, Brazil, South Africa and India. He authored 12 books on police procedure and criminal justice, co-authored *Community Policing: How to Get Started* and is still regarded as one of the leading academics in law enforcement.

As a leading scholar and director of the National Center for Community Policing, Trojanowicz emphasized the relational nature of policing. His objective was to bridge the gap between the police and the citizens, making officers more approachable and accountable to the communities they serve, often through increased foot or bicycle patrols. Robert Trojanowicz was a key figure in the development of community policing, contributing significantly through his early research and conceptualization of the philosophy, especially in the 1970s and 1980s. He co-authored influential works that provided a historical overview of community policing and highlighted its necessity, emphasizing community-police partnership and a proactive, problem-solving approach. His work helped lay the conceptual foundation for the broader adoption of community policing as a strategy to improve police-community relations and reduce crime. His 1974 work with Dixon was a groundbreaking discussion on the necessity of community policing and its potential to improve police-community relations. He co-authored a book with Bucqueroux that provided an important historical overview of community policing, explaining its roots and the community groups that were the focus of early initiatives. Trojanowicz's definition of community policing emphasized a "proactive reliance on community resources that seeks to change crime-causing conditions" through a problem-solving approach, which was a departure from the traditional, reactive law enforcement model. He advocated for a partnership between the police and the community to improve the quality of life and make the police more responsive to community needs. His contributions provided a crucial theoretical and historical foundation for the community policing movement that gained wider adoption in the late 20th century.

Theories and Their Objectives

The key theories underpinning community policing share common objectives related to community engagement, social dynamics, and organizational change:

Theory	Key Objective
Normative Sponsorship Theory	To involve the community in shaping policing norms and priorities, which in turn fosters trust and enhances effectiveness by ensuring police actions align with community values.
Social Resource Theory	To leverage social capital and community engagement for effective crime prevention. This theory views police as a social resource meant to address public concerns and build stronger, more cohesive communities.
Critical Social Theory	To use a critical lens to analyze and critique policing strategies within broader social, economic, and political contexts. The objective is to address systemic inequalities and work toward systemic transformation within law enforcement to ensure equitable treatment.

Table 5.1

Overarching Objectives of Community Policing

The collective objectives of these thinkers and theories manifest in the following goals for community policing initiatives:

- Build strong, collaborative relationships with community members, local businesses, non-profits, and other government agencies to jointly address public safety concerns.
- Actively work with residents to identify and resolve issues, leading to tangible reductions in criminal activity and increased public safety and quality of life.
- Encourage officers to be more accountable to the specific communities they serve, thereby improving perceptions of law enforcement legitimacy and the public's willingness to cooperate.

- Empower community members by involving them in problem-solving and decision-making processes, promoting a collective responsibility for public safety.
- Move beyond merely reacting to incidents to proactively identify and address the underlying social issues (e.g., lack of housing, mental health needs, poverty) that contribute to criminal activity.

For further information and resources, the US Department of Justice's Office of Community Oriented Policing Services is a primary resource.

Key thinkers in community policing include Sir Robert Peel, who established the foundation of crime prevention through community cooperation, and John Alderson, who focused on community policing principles and individual freedom. Other influential figures include Robert Trojanowicz and David Bucqueroux, who defined community policing as a partnership between the police and the citizens to solve local problems, and Robert Friedmann, who provided a comprehensive definition that includes community resources and accountability. Considered the father of modern democratic policing, he aimed to gain public cooperation and prioritize crime prevention by embedding officers in the community to build relationships, developed principles of community policing that emphasized the guarantee of personal freedom and free passage alongside a focus on community-based problem-solving, defined community policing as a shift in philosophy where the police and the citizens collaborate to solve problems like crime, social disorder, and neighborhood decay. Their work was geared toward the practical implementation of community policing strategies.

Robert Friedmann articulated a comprehensive definition of community policing as a strategy to achieve more effective crime control, reduce fear of crime, and improve the quality of life by proactively using community resources. He emphasized the need for greater police accountability and public involvement in decision-making.

Radhakrishnan implemented a community policing experiment in Trichy, India, with the core objectives of resolving communal problems and building public trust, particularly by addressing high crime rates and the fear of lawlessness.

Partnership and Collaboration: To shift from a reactive to a proactive policing model by fostering a partnership between the police and the community to address crime and disorder jointly.

Problem-solving: To move beyond simply reacting to crime and instead work with the community to identify the root causes of crime and disorder and develop solutions. Robert Trojanowicz was a prominent expert in community policing who, along with Bonnie Bucqueroux, argued that this approach fostered quality police-community relationships through increased communication and collaboration. His work highlighted the shift from a traditional, reactive policing model to one that emphasizes police-community partnerships to proactively address the underlying causes of crime and disorder. The core introduction to Trojanowicz's philosophy on "Building Police-Community Partnerships" centers on several key principles: the philosophy emphasizes that the police alone cannot solve all crime and social disorder problems. The public must accept their share of responsibility for the overall quality of life in their community, working in concert with law enforcement. Establishing and maintaining mutual trust is a central goal. This trust is built through open, regular communication and community outreach programs that increase transparency and accountability in police operations. Instead of merely reacting to incidents after they occur, the community policing approach focuses on identifying and analyzing the root causes of problems (problem-oriented policing) and on developing preventive strategies to address them. This involves police officers actively engaging with community members through activities such as foot patrols and neighborhood meetings to address locally specific issues and improve public safety. The ultimate objective extends beyond crime reduction; it aims to enhance the overall quality of life and reduce crime-related fear for all residents. Trojanowicz's work positioned community policing as a foundational philosophy for modern democratic policing, advocating a long-term strategic approach grounded in respect for human rights, accountability, and effective partnerships between the police and the communities they serve. It focuses on community engagement strategies, neighborhood foot patrols, and the importance of police-citizen trust.

Concluding Comments

Robert Trojanowicz, a key figure in the community policing movement, emphasized that building police-community partnerships is not a specific program but a comprehensive philosophy and organizational strategy that requires fundamental changes within police agencies and the community. His concluding comments and future direction for this approach focused on its long-term, systemic nature, the need for deep integration, and the potential to build stronger communities. Trojanowicz's work, often in collaboration with Bonnie Bucqueroux, highlighted that the community policing philosophy should be fully embraced rather than treated as a temporary initiative. Key conclusions included: He argued that community policing should replace traditional, reactive policing as the core function of law enforcement, moving beyond the idea of "police-community relations" or team policing programs. The central goal is to establish and maintain mutual trust and respect between officers and citizens, an essential foundation for any successful partnership. Effective partnerships require empowering community members to become active participants in identifying and solving local problems, not just being passive recipients of police services. He advocated decentralizing police services, such as through community police centers, to foster closer, continuous contact with the public, though later evaluations showed the need to better integrate these centers into core operations.

Future Direction

The future direction envisioned by Trojanowicz involved the total integration of this philosophy into the police culture and a greater focus on preventive measures. Future directions for the approach include: The process must be continuous and systematic, involving preparatory, implementation, evaluation, and modification stages across the entire agency, from individual officer behavior to overall strategy. The community is broadly defined to include non-profits, local businesses, and other government agencies; the future involves leveraging these diverse partnerships to address complex social problems effectively. The future direction included a call for rigorous evaluation of community policing outcomes beyond mere public popularity, assessing tangible impacts on crime rates, fear of crime, and community cohesion. Trojanowicz emphasized that community policing is a long-term strategic approach, not a short-term fix for immediate crises. Its success depends on sustained commitment to ongoing communication and relationship-building.

Overview

Trojanowicz's legacy emphasizes that effective public safety is a shared responsibility, requiring continuous, transparent, and collaborative efforts between law enforcement and the communities they serve.

Chapter 6 | COMPARATIVE POLICING MODELS

David H. Bayley

David H. Bayley, a leading international comparative policing scholar, did not propose a single, fixed set of "four models" of policing in a prescriptive sense. Instead, his work focused on analyzing the variability, structure, and effectiveness of police systems worldwide, examining how historical, cultural, and political contexts shape policing practices. His key contributions to comparative policing include: Bayley's research, notably in his book *Patterns of Policing: A Comparative International Analysis*, highlighted the great variation in police structures and behavior globally, even among modern democracies. He noted that while police forces worldwide tend to be public, focus on crime fighting, and be professionally trained, their organization and relationship with the public vary significantly, from centralized systems to the highly decentralized approach in the United States. In Police for the Future, Bayley presented the controversial thesis that police, in fact, cannot and do not effectively prevent most crime through traditional methods. He argued that a significant amount of police work involves maintaining order and providing services, rather than just crime-fighting. This conclusion led him to advocate for reforms focused on how police use their resources and interact with the community. In *Changing the Guard: Developing Democratic Police Abroad*, Bayley outlined several critical elements necessary for building democratic and effective police forces in developing countries, which are applicable globally. Rather than defining distinct "models" for universal application, David Bayley's work provides a framework for understanding that policing is a product of its societal context. He advocated for continuous assessment and reform to ensure that police are effective and accountable, and to build public trust through fair and transparent practices, regardless of the specific organizational structure.

David H. Bayley is a prominent scholar and author who has made significant contributions to the theory, practice, and critique of community policing. He has researched and published extensively on police systems around the world, particularly in the United States, Japan, and Singapore. On May 10, 2020, David Bayley's life came full circle: he died near Granville, close to where he was born 87 years earlier. He lived a full, meaningful life that took him far and wide before he retired several years ago at Kendal at Granville. He attended Denison University in Granville, where he met Anita "Chris" Ellis, his wife of 57 years; Chris died in 2014. Together they raised two daughters, and the whole family often travelled internationally for extended trips to university. He was a professor of criminal justice first at the University of Denver and then at the State University of New York at Albany, where he was the Dean of the School of Criminal Justice and a Distinguished Emeritus Professor who was highly respected for his superlative teaching and mentoring. He was the author of eighteen well-regarded scholarly books and many journal articles. His academic work became the practical foundation for promoting fair and democratic policing. He was also involved in creating new policing policies in the aftermath of political conflict in Bosnia and Northern Ireland. His passion was creating policing policies that relied on building community ties and minimizing coercion. He received international honors for his decades of contribution to the field, including the Order of the

Rising Sun, Golden Rays with Neck Ribbon from the government of Japan. He was a Fulbright Scholar at Oxford University and returned to Cambridge to supervise students doing research in policing. His circle of colleagues around the globe became his extended family, who often visited one another. He served as an active member of the Board of Trustees at Denison University for 25 years and helped navigate several major decisions. He was delighted to return to Granville for retirement, where he once again enjoyed attending plays and concerts as well as meeting with colleagues for scholarly discussions. He was active in several roles at Kendal at Granville. David H. Bayley was a leading international scholar of comparative policing models, focusing on how historical context, political structures, and culture shape police organizations and their effectiveness. His work emphasizes the variations in policing systems around the world and their impact on public safety and democratic governance.

Key Works and Comparisons

Bayley's primary comparative analyses can be found in several influential books:

- Forces of Order: Police Behaviour in Japan and the United States (1976)
- Patterns of Policing: A Comparative International Analysis (1985)
- Police for the Future (1994), which examines policing in Australia, Canada, Great Britain, Japan, and the United States
- Governing the Police: Experience in Six Democracies (co-authored)

Central Themes in Bayley's Comparative Research

Bayley's research highlights key differences and commonalities in policing across nations:

- Structure and Centralization: He notes a major variation in the structure of police forces, which are often either highly centralized (as in Japan) or decentralized (as in the United States, with its thousands of separate forces). He suggests the degree of centralization often relates to a government's perceived need for internal control. His work often explores the distinction between "policing by consent," in which police legitimacy is rooted in public approval and cooperation (often associated with the British model and Japan's koban system), and "policing by law," which emphasizes formal rules and legal authority. Bayley compares the primary functions of police forces, noting that while most public forces globally focus on "crime fighting," their reliance on non-emergency services and community engagement varies significantly by country. A core element of his later work is the study of "democratic policing," which defines systems in which police are accountable to the public and operate within the bounds of human rights and civil liberties. He identifies key elements necessary for developing democratic police abroad, such as procedural fairness and independent oversight. Bayley has critically analyzed what police can realistically achieve, famously arguing in *Police for the Future* that police alone do not and cannot prevent most crime. He stresses the importance of community mobilization and robust accountability mechanisms for police effectiveness and legitimacy.

Ultimately, Bayley's comparative models demonstrate that policing systems develop within unique socio-cultural backgrounds, meaning "best practices" cannot simply be transplanted from one nation to another without considering the local context.

Comparative Approach

David Bayley was a political scientist who provided a unique, comparative perspective on police governance and accountability, informed by his 65-year career and research across multiple countries. This article analyzes recent police reform proposals in the

US following the killing of George Floyd and the subsequent Black Lives Matter and "Defund the Police" movements, by evaluating them against Bayley's extensive work and his final book, *Governing the Police: Experience in Six Democracies.* Bayley's work drew on international comparative policing, looking at how different democratic nations govern their police forces. His work focused on governance and accountability. His scholarship centered on how police forces are governed and held accountable, a topic that remains relevant in the US today. The article frames the current debate in the US in the context of events such as George Floyd's death, which sparked renewed calls for reform. The author examines contemporary police reform ideas through the lens of Bayley's lifelong thoughts, culminating in his final co-authored book, *Governing the Police: Experience in Six Democracies.*

David H. Bayley was a leading international scholar of comparative policing models and a political scientist who became the world's preeminent expert in international policing studies. He focused on police governance, accountability, and the role of policing in democracy, and his work spanned over 60 years, influencing both his native US and numerous other countries, as well as international peace-keeping operations. Bayley taught at the University of Denver and the State University of New York at Albany, and was the dean of SUNY Albany's School of Criminal Justice from 1995 to 2004. He was known for his research on police governance and accountability in various countries and in the context of international peace-keeping operations. His work also explored the role of policing in democratic societies. Bayley was described as a "policing research pioneer" and one of the most respected experts in his field. He authored 18 books and was recognized as a leading authority for decades. Bayley's work, particularly his last book, *Governing the Police: Experience in Six Democracies*, continues to be referenced in discussions about police reform, especially following events like the death of George Floyd.

Key Thinkers and Their Models

The community policing philosophy is largely attributed to the work of thinkers such as Sir Robert Peel, Robert Trojanowicz, Malcolm Sparrow, and Wesley Skogan. They developed key models that compare and contrast traditional law enforcement with community-centric approaches, primarily the Traditional (Professional) Model and the Community-Oriented Policing (COP) Model.

- **Sir Robert Peel:** Often considered the "father of modern policing," his principles for the London Metropolitan Police Force in 1829 laid the foundation for "policing by consent," a core tenet of community policing. His model emphasized building public trust and cooperation, viewing the police as members of the community they serve, not a separate force.
- **Robert Trojanowicz and Bonnie Bucqueroux,** the co-founders of the National Center for Community Policing at Michigan State University, provided a well-known definition and perspective on community policing. Their model focused on decentralization, empowering frontline officers, and developing partnerships with the community to address the root causes of crime and disorder.
- **Wesley Skogan:** He identified the core elements of the community policing model as citizen involvement, problem solving, and decentralization. Skogan's work emphasizes community policing as an organizational strategy that enables residents and local officers to set priorities and achieve safety goals.
- **Malcolm Sparrow:** Sparrow, a professor at Harvard's Kennedy School of Government, contributed significantly to the related concept of Problem-Oriented Policing (POP). POP is often integrated with COP, focusing on systematic problem analysis and innovative solutions rather than just responding to incidents.

Comparative Policing Models

The shift in policing theory is often described through three historical eras: the Political Era, the Reform (Professional) Era, and the Community Era.

Feature	Traditional/Professional Model (Reform Era)	Community-Oriented Policing(COP) Model (Community Era)
Philosophy	Law enforcement is a reactive "force" separate from the community, focused on responding to incidents and making arrests.	Law enforcement is a "service" that is integrated into the community, focused on proactive problem-solving and prevention.
Structure	Centralized, hierarchical command structure; officers follow orders from the top.	Decentralized decision-making; field officers are empowered to identify and solve local problems in consultation with residents.
Role of Citizens	Citizensarepassiverecipientsofpoliceservicesandsourcesofinformation/witnesses.	Citizens are active partners in identifying problems, developing strategies, and taking responsibility for neighbourhood safety (e.g., Neighborhood Watch programs).
Effectiveness Measures	Primarily measured by crime rates, response times, and arrest numbers.	Measured by reduced fear of crime, improved quality of life, increased citizen satisfaction, and enhanced police legitimacy and trust.

Table 6.1

The SARA Model for Problem-Solving

A core practical model used within community policing is SARA, an outgrowth of problem-oriented policing, which stands for:

- **Scanning:** Identifying recurring community problems.
- **Analysis:** Researching the underlying causes and conditions that create the problem.
- **Response:** Developing and implementing solutions tailored to the specific problem.

- **Assessment:** Evaluating the effectiveness of the responses and making adjustments.

Community Policing in Comparative Perspective

Policing is one of the most important functions undertaken by every sovereign government. In the state machinery, the police are an indispensable organ that maintains law and order and serves as the first link in the criminal justice system. On the other hand, for the common people, the police force is a symbol of brute authority and, at the same time, a protector against crime. Police men get a corporate identity from the uniform they wear; the common person identifies, distinguishes and awes them on account of the same uniform. The police systems across the world have developed in a socio-cultural background, and for this reason alone, huge differences exist between these police systems. From the singular coordinated centralized system of police in Saudi Arabia, organized under the Ministry of Interior, to the 42000 odd police forces that exist in the USA, policing mainly rests on either of the two broad principles:

- Policing by consent and
- Policing by law

The role of a modern police organization is succinctly laid out in the quote above, which appears on the UK Home Office website. The first idea that comes to our mind when we hear the term "Police" is the idea of a dominant personality who symbolizes the power of the State and criminal justice administration system. On the one hand, people view police as a protector of civil liberties and on the other hand, police are viewed as a symbol of the brute force of the state, which oppresses legitimate protests with force. It represents the presence of the civil body politic in everyday life. It conveys a sense of power or sacredness that lies at the root of political order. It represents the means by which the political authorities maintain the status quo. It represents the capacity of the state to deter citizens from committing acts that threaten the order they are believed to symbolize. It gives a corporate identity to the police men. The authority of police comes from the people- their laws and institutions. Police agencies are not only part of the community but also part of the government, which determines their formal base of authority and the criminal justice system, which determines society's course in deterring lawbreakers and rehabilitating offenders. In a Constitutional system, the ultimate authority springs from the Constitution itself. The authority of police in every jurisdiction is derived from the sovereign authority- it can be either the Constitution, which gives the elected government executive authority over the subjects, or the "grund norm", which gives the sovereign authority over its subjects, devoid of any written constitution.

Different Models of Policing

The organization of police across countries is primarily rooted in each country's socio-cultural and historical background. For example, in a country like the UK, with a long tradition of parliamentary democracy, policing works on the principle of consent by the population, whereas in most other countries, policing power is vested in the state by law. As such, police organizations in many countries have nothing in common except their basic goals (in some jurisdictions, even these goals do not match). However, criminologists have sought to identify common features of police structures worldwide, focusing on the most prominent one: the command architecture.

This model classification is based on two dimensions:

- Classification based on legitimacy or legal backing of police function:
  - ✓ Policing by consent,
  - ✓ Policing by law.
- Classification based on command structure:
  - ✓ Centralized
  - ✓ Decentralized
  - ✓ Single/Singular

Number of Forces to be Commanded

If the entire police force in a country is organized as a single force under a single commander, the model is called the singular model; if, in a single country, there are multiple police forces, as in India, it is called the multiple model. Within the multiple models, if police forces have well-defined territories of operation and their functions do not overlap, the model is called Multiple Coordinated; if the reverse is true, as in India, where many agencies can have overlapping jurisdictions, it is called Multiple Uncoordinated.

Typeof Forces

If the police forces in a country are highly organized and have a centralized command, it is called a coordinated centralized police force, and if the police forces in a country do not have an apparent centralized command structure, it is called a decentralized command structure.

Comparative Study of Police Systems

Saudi Arabia

Saudi Arabia is a typical model of a centralized, coordinated police force with a single line of command emanating from the King. Both the Minister of Interior and the Director of Public Safety are appointed by the King, and both are usually senior members of the King's family itself. The Police, known as Public Security police, is responsible for general policing throughout the country and derives its authority from Executive Orders and the Shariah. Public Security Police is divided into Regular Police and Special Investigative Police (SIP), known as "Mubahit". Regular Police is directly under the control of the Ministry of Interior, and is run by the Director of Public Safety. In contrast, SIP operates under the control of the General Directorate of Investigation (GIP) and is responsible for criminal investigations and for managing domestic security and counterintelligence functions. In addition to the Public Security Police, there is also a religious police called Mutawwiun, which is directly under the King, and whose main duty is enforcement of Islamic Shariah. Since Mutawwiun generally takes the form of a religious band and is not responsible for general law-and-order maintenance functions, it is more a religious sect than a police force. Except for the Mutawwiun, the police force is organized as a single unit in Saudi Arabia.

While this is the general picture of policing in Saudi Arabia, there are jurisdictional pockets of tribal authority in Saudi Arabia, which are beyond the reach of even the King's justice. In the tribal pockets, the tribal elders are a law unto themselves and do not tolerate interference from external authorities. So, law-and-order or criminal investigation issues in these pockets are handled by the tribal elders themselves, with the regular police providing tactical support wherever required. One important feature of the Saudi Police System is that the line distinguishing the Saudi Regular Armed forces and Police is very narrow, and the policing functions are often supported by the Saudi National Guard and the armed forces.

China

China is another example of a singularly coordinated, centralized police force. The Ministry of Public Security (MPS) is a functional organization under the State Council responsible for public security nationwide. Public security departments are set in provinces and autonomous regions; metropolitan public security bureaus are set in direct municipalities; public security bureaus or divisions are assigned to cities and prefectures; sub-bureaus are set in sub-regions of cities, under the direct leadership of their superior public security agencies; public security bureaus are set in counties and banners, under the leadership of their respective local government and superior public security agencies. Dispatched police stations are directly subordinate to their superior public security bureaus and sub-bureaus at the county and banner levels.

France

France is a typical example of a police force with a multi-coordinated, centralized structure. France has two national law enforcement agencies:

- Police Nationale, formerly called the Sûreté, a civilian force, with primary responsibility in urban areas and run under the Ministry of the Interior.
- Gendarmerie Nationale, a gendarmerie, with primary responsibility in rural areas and military installations and run under the Ministry of Defence and under operational control, for most purposes, of the Ministry of the Interior.

Apart from these two, there are other agencies, such as the Direction générale des douanes et droits indirects, a civilian customs service more commonly known as the "Douane", under the Minister of Budget, Public Accounting and Civil Servants. French municipalities may also have a local police force called the Police municipale, Garde municipale, or Garde champetre, with restricted powers: they can only enforce municipal by-laws.

The United Kingdom

The United Kingdom (UK), which comprises England, Scotland, Wales and Northern Ireland, is the world's oldest democracy and policing in the UK also grew from the principle of "policing by consent". Even though the basic premise of policing in the UK is consent-based, the British Police system as it exists now is more a process of law, granting more power to people than policing by consent. As such, policing in the UK has now become policing by law, but a law that mandates the police and holds them accountable to the public. The UK is a typical example of a multiple-coordinated, decentralized police force. The UK does not have a national police service but a network of 43 individual police forces responsible for policing specific counties, cities, or areas, excluding those with special jurisdiction. These 43 forces comprise more than 140,500 police officers, 14,000 volunteer special constables, and 13,400 community support officers. The UK has a three-way system of responsibility that ensures the smooth running of forces. The Home Office funds the police and has the overall responsibility as overseer and coordinator of the police forces. Police authorities ensure local forces operate efficiently and effectively. Chief Police Officers have responsibility for the direction and control of regional forces. According to the UK Home Office, this system prevents political interference in policing and avoids giving any single organization power over the entire police service. In addition, there is an independent Police Complaints Authority and an Inspectorate of Constabulary. While the Police Complaints Commission examines complaints against police officials, the Inspectorate of Constabulary acts as an audit wing of the police, examining and assessing the efficiency of the police. The Police Reforms Act, 2002 requires the Home Secretary to prepare an annual Policing Plan and to place it before the legislature. The budgetary control of each police force rests with the Police Authority, which consists of at least 17 members. There is representation for local elected representatives, the judiciary and the common people. In every police authority, such representation includes nominations from the Home Office as well as members selected through an open recruitment process. All bodies, such as the Inspectorate of Constabulary, the Independent Police Complaints Authority, and Police Authorities, function as independent bodies with a separate corporate identity distinct from that of the police.

Spain

Spain is a typical example of a multiple, uncoordinated, centralized police force. As in almost all European Countries, policing is based on the principle of "Policing by law". The system is called a multiple, centralized, uncoordinated force because there is more than one police force in the country, but at the top, they all report to the same authority. The authority of these forces overlaps in many places. In conformity with the Constitution, the organic law on law enforcement bodies defines the structure of public safety in Spain.

Under the Spanish constitution, public safety is the responsibility of the State alone, and the national Government's role is to maintain security. Autonomous communities and local corporations may participate, through their own security forces, in the law-and-order maintenance and crime investigation functions of the police. Spain has a National Police, a civilian force that operates primarily in urban areas. The Guardia Civil (Civil Guard) is a military force that operates mainly in rural areas. Local communities have either units of police forces attached to their executives or their own police forces.

The United States of America

There is no national police force in the US; policing is organized at the state and local levels. The country has around 500,000 police officers and a total of 40,000 separate police forces, over half of which are simply one or two-person sheriffs' offices in small towns. In addition to regular full-time police officers, many towns have auxiliary, part-time police officers, special duty and volunteer sheriff's posses (which assist sheriffs' offices in some areas). Law enforcement in the United States is decentralized. Federal authorities address violations of federal law within their respective jurisdictions. There are approximately 65 different federal police agencies. At the local level, each of the 50 sovereign states has its own state legislature that enacts criminal statutes under its state constitution. Most of the US States have police at all levels – municipal, county and state levels.

Specific Organizational features of police vary greatly from small, informally organized departments with 2-3 employees to highly organized metropolitan departments with numerous subdivisions and thousands of employees. Police structures vary greatly among and within the federal, state and local levels. The primary responsibility of policing is at the local level, while state-level officials have only specific duties.

India

India has the most police personnel in the world, with 1,032,960. The USA has the second-largest police force in the world, with 941,139 police officers. The UK and France come 9th and 10th, respectively. However, considering the population of the country, India has only 0.956207 per 1,000 people and comes 47th in the world, while the UK, with 2.04871 per 1,000 people, stands at 34th position. The Indian model of police organization is an example of a multi-unorganized, decentralized policing system. In sharp contrast to the British principle of policing by consent, India follows policing by law. Each state has its own police force, whose top echelons are filled by officers of the Indian Police Service, which is a central service. Many analysts have commented that the Indian Police Act, 1861, which was brought into force immediately after the First War of Indian Independence in 1857, was based on distrust of Indian officials and was aimed at ensuring strict control over the Indian population. Even after attaining independence, successive governments did not try to change this basic character of the Indian Police Force. Though the framers of the Indian Constitution envisaged police as a state subject, vide Article 246 read with entries I & 2 of List II of Seventh Schedule of Indian Constitution, most Indian states opted to adopt the Indian Police Act, 1861 without any change, while the very few states, including Kerala which opted for Police Act of its own, modeled its statute broadly based on the Indian Police Act, 1861 itself. Even the Model Police Act, 2008, does not differ significantly from the philosophy of the Indian Police Act, 1861. While we can broadly classify the Indian Police organization as a multi-tier, uncoordinated, decentralized model, the presence of IPS officers at the top ranks of most police forces creates an oblique Form of Centralized control. The quasi-federal character of the Indian polity, with specific provisions in the Constitution, allows the Centre to play a coordinating and counselling role in police matters and even authorizes it to set up certain central police organizations.

The head of the police force in each state is the Director General of Police (DGP), responsible to the state government for the administration of the police force and for advising the government on police matters. The DGP represents the highest rung in the police hierarchy. The hierarchical structure of the police in India follows a vertical alignment consisting of senior officers drawn, by and large, from The Indian Police Service (IPS) who do the supervisory work, the "upper subordinates" (inspectors, sub-inspectors, and asst. sub-inspectors) who work generally at the police station level, and the police constabulary who are delegated the patrolling, surveillance, guard duties, and law and order work—the constabulary accounts for almost 88% of the total police strength.

Section 3 of the Police Act, 1861, vested the state government with the superintendence of the state police force. A system of dual control at the district level is introduced under Sec.4 of the Indian Police Act, 1861. It puts the police forces under the District Superintendent of Police, but they remain under the overall control and direction of the District Magistrate. The draft Police Act, 2008, apparently tries to change this dual control.

Community Policing and Traditional Policing: A Comparative Analysis

The police force is a government service charged with the responsibility of maintaining law and order and ensuring public safety throughout. For more than three centuries of modern policing, the task of defining the role of the police and the extent of their discretionary powers has been a continuous subject of debate. This debate has taken place at various levels, including among the police themselves, in the political arena, and in the public forum. And this debate has manifested an important disparity in the way police officers perform their duties and the nature of their interactions with the citizens that they serve. This disparity is the foundation of community policing and is in profound contrast to the known practices of modern police work. It is the intent of this paper to show the contrast in the data available, reflecting the disparity between how police work is done today and how it used to be done, with a movement back to a more traditional community-based approach to addressing the needs of the public. Community policing represents a means to reform the police. It is not a single approach but rather a general orientation towards the police function that encompasses a variety of strategies, including decentralization, de-emphasizing law enforcement as the only solution to crime, and developing positive police-community relations. Community policing rests on the belief that the law alone cannot secure public compliance and that the law has no validity without the support of the vast majority of citizens. According to the US Department of Justice, community policing is a philosophy that promotes organizational strategies that systematically use partnerships and problem-solving techniques to proactively address the immediate conditions that give rise to public safety issues, such as crime, social and physical disorder, and fear of crime. The book focuses on the background of each style and describes the strategies employed in both models—the core aspect of both practices, i.e., how effective they are in practice. The main body of the essay will compare and contrast the effectiveness of both styles and state what may be the most effective route for policing. All information will be gathered from a collection of books and online resources, and all sources will be included in a full bibliography at the end of the assignment. With the development of a new style of policing, it is hard to say which method is more effective, though community policing appears to yield many positive results. This may be because it can gain trust from the public, encouraging them to work with the police. This can only be described as a positive move, as it can only make the area a better place if the police and public work together. The areas where community policing has been tried and the studies conducted show that CP is a positive move, and in some areas, the crime rate has reduced from what it was under traditional policing. This may be illustrated by the statement that traditional policing's methods of "crack down" on an area can cause tensions between the police and the public when actions are disputable. High crime rates and significant social disorder in communities across the nation have left many law enforcement agencies with only one choice: do something different in these communities in terms of policing.

Community Policing and Traditional Policing

In the history of the United States, especially over the past 20 years, police departments have succeeded and failed in certain areas of policing, eventually changing their plans and strategies to better serve the community and the department. These are broken down into two different policing strategies: community policing and traditional or problem-oriented policing. Although many today say that community policing is merely a philosophy rather than a strategy, in this essay, I will identify how adopting a community policing model improves police strategies and police-public relations, thereby advancing the greater good of the community and the department. Traditional policing has clinched the title for being the model of what a police department should be. This is due to tradition. Since the early 1900s, society and the police department have associated policing with a professional force in a crime-fighting era. The aim was to reduce crime rates and create a safer community. It was to this effect that the police were to serve the community. This was at least the ideology when Sir Robert Peel founded the community in London's metropolitan area. Peel's ideology has been closely followed and passionately embraced by many departments in the 20th century. Peel also identified the definition of the police at that time: Sherlock Holmes. This, along with many other atmospheric conditions, has led to the belief that the police are crime fighters who deal only with criminals and should maintain a professional attitude. This belief still holds strong in today's society. The police are always under the microscope, as the public demands that they live up to professional standards and fight crime to the fullest. This has led to the deployment of speciality units and an emphasis on police activity in lower-class/slum areas where crime rates are high (Trojanowicz, 1998, p. 3). The reason for this is the basic way criminal justice is defined: we define a problem and go to its source with the intent of eradicating it. This is a reactive form of policing.

Community Policing Principles and Practices

Community policing represents a new interpretation of the police role, one which encourages police initiative, innovation, and a proactive stance in solving community problems. The use of community policing in America has raised questions and concerns. Now that this has been tried and found effective, the questions stem from what community policing is and how it works. This paper attempts to provide some answers. First, by exploring the concept of community policing, what it is, the ideas that lie behind it, and how it differs from other policing tactics. Following this, we will take a look at the key elements of community policing to answer what makes it unique. Finally, we will have a look at how communities are involved in community policing. This paper discusses the utilization of community policing ideals in an anti-terrorism environment. Although concerns remain over the potential weapon that community policing provides to terrorists and the exploitation of community policing strategies to gather intelligence on community members, the paper suggests that properly performed, community policing strategies can reduce the occurrence of terror acts and minimize the damage caused by such acts.

Definition and Concept of Community Policing

The term "community" is so loaded that it means different things to different people. The only common thread is that the word "community" implies the presence of more than one person. The Oxford English Dictionary's first definition of community is "The condition of having certain attitudes and interests in common." Perhaps the most significant definition of community is "a group of people residing in the same area under the same government," which is strongly supported by Rousseau's identification of community with government. Rousseau goes on to specify the word community as "a real social order, uniting all members of a society under common laws for the general welfare and prosperity." This is the communitarian idea of community - from which community policing stems - that suggests a partnership between the formal institutions of government and the functional community, which desires order maintenance and the ability to resolve its persistent social problems. This stems from yet another definition of community: a community may also be a shared environment. In its broadest sense, this can be a city or a town; in a social-psychological sense, it can be a residential neighborhood. But no matter the definition, it is generally accepted that communities are social units concerned only with the welfare of a particular population. This distinction is important because community, within the context of community policing, does not mean the same thing as society, whose welfare is focused on the state, the federal government, or international issues. It is concerned with the welfare of a particular population, particularly as it relates to public safety issues. This idea of community is consistent with the current social organization of the criminal justice system, in that a jurisdiction (municipal court, county sheriff's dept., state police, etc.) is viewed as a protector and service provider for a particular population.

Principles of Community Policing

Leraby and Peyrefitte categorize community policing into three types - preventive, community, and problem-solving policing - suggesting that the first two types concentrate on the re-establishment of the partnership that is said to have been lost in the last 30 years, rather than a partnership that has never existed. Alternatively, Trojanowicz and Bucqueroux (1990) identify 11 principles of community policing, advocating a less offense-specific approach that emphasizes a long-term, family-like commitment to the community. These principles are: change from reaction to pro-action, decentralization, empowerment, more effective prevention and problem resolution, changed police role, and improved quality of life. This essay will apply the more modern eight Peelian principles of policing to the principles by Trojanowicz and Bucqueroux, stating that both parties have the same vision of a community-based ideal state in contrast to today's society, and in doing so will compare and contrast the concept of community policing in relation to the police role and their influence on the community. The first principle of community policing, according to Trojanowicz and Bucqueroux, is to change from reaction to pro-action. This is similar to the final Peelian principle, which holds that the police are the public and the public are the police, specifically focusing on the prevention of crime in communities.

The Role of Community in Community Policing

Community policing recognizes the valuable role of the community in public safety and in the policing process. It is predicated on the use of proactive, information-based problem-solving methodologies and recognizes the need for police to work in partnership with the community. The basic premise is to prevent crime and maintain order by reducing citizens' fear of crime and providing them with a safer environment in which to live. Central to this is a greater willingness on the part of the community to engage in the policing of their neighborhood. This ranges from providing greater assistance and support to their local police to taking on more responsibility for activities aimed at crime prevention and enhancing the community's overall safety and security. An important element of this is for the police to consult with the community and ensure they understand the community's needs and concerns regarding crime and safety. This can range from open community meetings to mere informal discussions with individuals in the community. From this, the police seek to identify the causes of crime and disorder that are most concerning to the community. This information is then used to plan and implement strategies to prevent this type of crime or disorder. By involving the community at this level, the police can ensure that their strategies are based on a relevant and accurate understanding of the problems affecting the community and are more likely to be supported by the community.

Traditional Policing: Methods and Approaches

Definition and Characteristics of Traditional Policing

Traditional policing can be considered the standard model used in the United States for policing. It is a description of the standard model and its functions, which explains the characteristics that distinguish it from the Community-Oriented Policing model.

Reactive Nature of Traditional Policing

This section explains the differences between traditional policing and community policing by comparing the preventive problem-solving techniques in community policing to the standard model response of incident-driven policing. The section explains what incident-driven or traditional policing is and why the reactive nature of traditional policing is discussed. It then, to better show what separates the two models, compares the two styles in terms of a recent increase in youth violence. It has been shown that during a time of economic hardship, the city of Collerville was considering cutting several recreation programs. The city council was made aware of a recent increase in youth violence and is pressured to keep the programs to prevent further violence. A community policing approach would investigate the causes of the violence and programs to prevent it, and focus on preserving the programs and benefiting the community. Traditional policing would serve as a short-term solution and prescribe more arrests of youth and possibly a curfew to reduce further violence. The reactive nature of incident-driven policing can be seen because violence would have to directly affect an area, scaling police deterrence to more serious crimes, and precipitating the increased youth arrests. Though the youth arrests would be an effective crime control method, public safety would not be increased, and the youth would be stigmatized as criminals. The decision to reinstate the programs would not have an effect on the recent youth violence, and it would be seen as a failure, leading to the termination of programs at a later date. An increase in the crime rate could result from the loss of programs in response to the council's decision to save face.

Definition and Characteristics of Traditional Policing

Traditional policing is based on the idea of protecting the community by apprehending criminals and deterring criminal activity. The community's role in this is simply to support the police in this job. Traditional policing looks at the police as only one segment in the criminal justice system. It is also a response to society, providing a service deemed a necessity. Over the years, the traditional model has been refined from a simple, reactive, incident-driven endeavor into a complex, proactive approach to preventing, solving, and controlling crime. The key characteristic of the traditional model is its hierarchical structure, in which it is clearly defined who is in command and who is to take orders. There is a narrow span of control, essential for maintaining a clear and direct line of supervision from higher-ranking officers to lower ranks. Training is an essential element in preparing police for fieldwork, and it has typically been conducted at designated institutions. Finally, the traditional model is based on values, such as efficiency, discipline, and uniformity.

Reactive Nature of Traditional Policing

The reactive nature of traditional policing is evident because police forces are mobilized only in response to public calls, and thus, they are only present in certain areas when direct action is required. This ensures that the reactive (problem-solving) work they carry out is the only crime-prevention work that takes place. As they are responsible for maintaining law and order, the lines between first-line response and community involvement have become blurred. Evidence of this can be found in the ever-increasing use of PCSOs, who, despite their civilian attire, are seen as a way to increase police presence. However, traditional police forces have always relied on the public to report incidents, which means much of their work is reactive. Evans and Newnham (1995) identify a 'hierarchy of response' in which the seriousness of the incident dictates the level of policing response. Incidents deemed to be of lesser severity will generate a response involving less qualified officers and, in some cases, civilians to undertake investigative work. This ideally will free up police officers to deal with matters affecting public safety. However, Newburn's (2012) work shows that reactive work by traditional police forces is often inefficient. This is largely due to a lack of resources, and high-profile crimes will often divert police personnel from preventive work to public reassurance.

Limitations of Traditional Policing

Functionalism and organizational theory, along with the study of US policing, are the two theoretical frameworks used to discuss the limitations of traditional policing. According to functionalists and organizational theorists, the principal mission of law enforcement is to investigate criminal activities and apprehend offenders. Enforcing the law is seen as maintaining the established norm and preventing any deviation from it. This is to be accomplished with limited use of force and by treating all citizens as equals. Only through enforcing the law can a moral order be established, and actions that are not defined as criminal need no regulation (Wilson and Kelling, 1982). These definitions are similar to traditional policing in that enforcement is directed primarily at low-income, marginalized communities to prevent and control crime. This method is limited in that it only deals with the symptoms of crime and not the underlying causes, preventing true crime control from being realized. Warren and McConnell (2006) list specific functions of law enforcement that are found in traditional policing. Many of these revolve around random preventive patrol and rapid response. The research literature has consistently shown that random preventive patrol is no more effective in reducing street crime than a control strategy that relies on the threat of arrest and the deterrent effects of severe sanctions in specific high-crime target areas. Directed patrol might be useful if focused on specific high-crime areas. However, today, downtown and other commercial areas are sometimes selected for foot or car patrols despite relatively low levels of violent and property crime. This seems to be a costly waste of police resources. Rapid response suffers from focusing on immediate reaction to incidents, rather than long-term achievement. According to the research, most incidents that police respond to are non-urgent, and a delayed response would have no consequences. This function also ties up police officers who could be more usefully employed elsewhere.

Comparative Analysis of Community Policing and Traditional Policing

Community policing is a strategy used by various police forces across the United States to build better relationships between the police and the communities they serve. By engaging the members of the community, the police are better able to get a sense of what the main concerns of the citizens are by identifying the problems and problem solvers. This enables the police and the community to identify and address the main concerns, leading to a safer environment. Traditional policing, which was used before the implementation of community policing, is a method focusing on police staying detached from the community and taking care of problems after the fact. This is done through routine patrols of an area to provide quick responses to calls and to show police presence to deter potential crime. While both are effective in their own ways, community policing is a more proactive strategy, as police work with the community to identify and solve problems, which can ultimately lead to fewer calls for police service in a safer environment.

Effectiveness in Crime Prevention and Reduction

Traditionally, the primary objective of the police force was to enforce laws, maintain order, and fight crime. In time, a 'reactionary' strategy materialized, one in which the police would respond to recent criminal activity within the community. Only recently has the idea of crime prevention been a factor in deciding police policy. Community policing has made a significant mark on contemporary policing strategies. One of the main objectives of community policing is to prevent/reduce crime activity. This is pursued by building relationships with community members and implementing strategies to deter various types of criminal activity. It is with this similar objective of crime prevention that traditional policing and community policing can be compared. Community policing was supplanted with the initial concept that community residents, not the police, are the key to crime prevention. Community policing has been structured in such a way that police officers, through consulting with local community leaders and residents, have been able to identify their main concerns in their respective communities. With this said, crime prevention strategies and intervention methods have been implemented on a community-specific basis. These methods are not limited to police action and involvement. At issue are strategies involving other public and/or private agencies, community residents, and community businesses (Thacher, 2001). In a recent study, it was posited that traditional policing and community policing do not have large enough differences in their strategies and methods to affect any significant change in crime prevention (Curry, 2008). Despite this, the study did find that community-specific methods of crime prevention had higher success rates in preventing certain types of crime. For example, a community drug intervention method would be more effective in preventing drug-related crime in a community as opposed to an anti-drug program that takes place somewhere with no specific community in mind.

Relationship Building and Trust with the Community

Relationship building and community trust are indispensable to police in demonstrating their legitimacy and to local communities in accepting the legitimacy of their social control. This is not only a concern for community policing but also for traditional policing. As Edwards and Harris pointed out: "Without community support, police would have great difficulty in carrying out their activities, no matter how well organized and equipped they are" (Edwards and Harris, 2007:51). Community policing has built this insight into its practice, aiming to address the problem of crime and disorder through proactive problem-solving activities and in partnership with the community. This is seen to contrast with a reactive model of law enforcement, where police simply respond to incidents of crime, isolated from the community, through investigations aimed at identifying a perpetrator and securing a conviction with a punitive sentence. Trust and confidence in the police are also seen as critical factors in the support required to implement policing initiatives, whether directed at the community or specific problems, and in communities' engagement in social crime prevention activities. A survey of Londoners found that: "Trust and confidence in the police affects the amount of formal social control and compliance with the law that an individual or community is subject to" (Morgan et al, 2007:8). This study for the Home Office indicated that increased trust and confidence in the police is associated with less unwanted social behavior and victimization. A lack of confidence that the police will deal with their issues seriously and sensitively is a reason given for minority communities not reporting hate crimes and incidents that are part of the harassment and victimization process. This is not just a matter of perception, as a study of the NYP's response to hate crime found that there was a lack of understanding in what constitutes hate incidents and crime and the differences between different forms of victimization, meaning that police response was often insensitive and inappropriate (Bowling et al, 2008). Confidence and trust in the police can be entrenched in some communities through historical legacies and entwinements between the forces of law and order and social groups. This can be a barrier to improving relations and to any attempts by the police to actually change policy and be given a chance. An example of this comes from research from North America that many African American communities have a deep-seated distrust of law enforcement, which stems from a history of slave patrols and the enforcement of segregation laws (Skolnick & Fyfe, 1993). This often translates to African Americans' perception of unfair or biased treatment by the police in the modern day.

Community policing (CP) is a philosophy and an organizational strategy that promotes a new partnership between the people and their police. It is based on the premise that, to build safer communities, police and citizens need to work together. It moves away from traditional policing, which is mainly reaction-based and most of the time responds to crime after it occurs. CP is proactive and involves problem-solving. Traditional policing methods are mostly focused on random patrol, rapid response to calls for service, and often investigative work after a crime has already occurred. Random patrols can be seen as a significant resource consumer relative to their effectiveness at preventing crime. Since much of it is directed at non-criminal events and involves minimal time spent in specific target areas, it is inefficient in preventing crime.

High visibility in a community is important, but it is most effective when patrolling has a clear focus, and the community sees the police addressing problems while also deterring crime. With traditional policing, there is an emphasis on rapid response to calls for service. This can allocate too large a proportion of resources to immediate or short-term situations, leaving limited resources to address ongoing community problems. Although response time is important in many situations, studies have shown that only 5-10% of calls require immediate police attention, and a lower response time does not affect the outcome. CP primarily employs a proactive problem-solving approach to identify and resolve community problems. It encourages the use of analysis and assessment tools to help target specific problems and track the effectiveness of the problem-solving efforts. This is done to ensure the most efficient use of resources and to prevent unnecessary allocation of resources to problems or specific locations where police impact is limited. In contrast to traditional policing, CP efforts are typically conducted in focused, small-team sessions in specific locations to address specific problems. These teams are often drawn from a wide range of police units and ranks to better understand the specific problem and its implications and to build problem-solving skills throughout the organization. The resources used in such efforts are as important as the personnel involved. It has been argued that traditional policing tends to throw money at crime problems with little consideration of resource allocation. This has been characterized by the sole use of increased levels of certain strategies, such as preventive patrols or crackdowns on particular crimes, with no increase in their effectiveness, and inflexible changes to resource allocations without consideration of problem analysis and potential alternative strategies.

The Models of Policing

During the colonial period, policing in the United States was also influenced by British models. In the South, however, slave patrols were formalized to regulate the movements and behaviors of enslaved populations. These groups were empowered to use extralegal forms of violence to enforce the will of plantation owners against the enslaved population. In the North and upper South, early policing centered on the control of urban and immigrant populations. Here, early forms of policing in the United States mirrored English models more closely. In the colonial period, homeowners and public officials were often required to take up arms, patrol the streets, and keep the peace. This system of constables and citizen cooperation led to the development of "watch" groups and "nightly patrols" composed of community volunteers tasked with maintaining order. When citizens were unable or unwilling to volunteer, local officials would conscript workers to police the streets at night. As cities grew and industry took hold of rural America, the public became disconnected and discontent with those men "press-ganged" or forced into service mainly because of their class, ethnicity, and economic status. Modern police forces in the United States emerged in response to disorder resulting from rapid industrialization and urbanization, and to a declining willingness of the citizenry to perform what they saw as onerous and potentially dangerous "night watch" duties. Posting the 13th Amendment in 1865 and a standing professional police force soon arising in the wake of the Civil War, the era of the "slave patrols" and "night watches" was ended. Policemen in the new metropolitan departments, with the full authority of the state at their backs - now backed by professional police organizations and political powers eager to modernize - focused on political and economic order. The modern police department was born. The evolution of American police and law-enforcement methods from the political era and into the present day has been as dynamic and evolutionary as the political, economic, and demographic changes that have shaped the country. American policing has undergone transformation through shifts in social and political contexts, technological innovation, changes in workforce composition, and evolving understandings of police accountability in maintaining order and preventing crime. The modernization of police forces and the more professional era we are currently in can be traced back to the "Progressive" movement of the 19th and 20th centuries, which sought to remove corrupt influences from government and to work toward a more "systemic" and "objective" form of governance. It was also during the Progressive Era that modern police practices, such as education and training, advances in automobile and communication technology, and other "innovations," were introduced. However, these advances in policing also saw an increasing reliance on technology and patrol cars. As the police became "automobile," patrolling vast areas of the city instead of "on foot" beat style policing that had defined the "political" era, the authorities began to distance themselves from maintaining close ties to the public, leading some scholars to argue that the police today are alienated from the citizenry and have become mere "guardians of the status quo."

Early Forms of Policing

The initial forms of policing in both the UK and the US in the 18th century began to resemble the criminal justice systems we recognize today. These early attempts at preserving law and order were not driven by detection and the resolution of crime, but to a certain extent by efforts to constrain and control the lives of the poor. The Metropolitan Police Force was established by Sir Robert Peel in 1829 and became the forerunner of contemporary urban policing in the UK. Peel aimed to create a well-ordered force with a system of command and disciplinary structure. It was identified by the so-called "Peelian Principles," which are still invoked today. The original principles served as ethical guidance for the very first Metropolitan police officers, and there is little doubt they helped establish a more forceful, less politically motivated police force. All patrol zones were accounted for, and the number of police officers in each zone could be easily compared with the number of reported crimes in that zone over a defined period. This is an example of an early successful demonstration of data being used for management purposes in policing.

Furthermore, the central government regularly issued orders, and numerous commissions of inquiry began investigating various grievances. This denotes the emergence of administrative freedom from local authority, another important feature of the modern police service. This period, towards the mid-19th century, marked the initiation of the transition towards the professionalization of policing in the UK. The formal, hierarchical procedures and the use of the military as police, such as in the "Horse Patrol" and the "Foot Patrol," were replaced by a knowledgeable, disciplined practice. The once-erratic, largely disreputable gangs and groups that were employed to some extent have largely stopped committing wrongdoing. Such impact was amplified by the common reputation and the forestalling apprehension towards the gangs, which, from such guise, helped drastically reduce crime and beliefs, accentuating the formidable operation of the initial forms of primary policing (Gardiner, 2011).

Evolution of Modern Policing Systems

Modern policing systems are the result of many actions and ideas that developed over time. In the early 19th century, the idea of "professional policing" began to take hold. With the Industrial Revolution, many people moved to cities to work in factories that were springing up across the industrialized world. There was work, but not everyone could find it, and some people turned to crime. Factories and their machinery were expensive, and factory owners were keen to protect their investments. The factory owners became the "victims" of the early crimes of the Industrial Revolution and were therefore the first to create organized police forces to prevent them; up until then, they had to pay for their own protection. The modern police force in the United Kingdom is a product of a political and public reform movement in the 19th century, which has been attributed to Sir Robert Peel.

In 1829, facing rising crime and social disorder, Home Secretary Sir Robert Peel proposed to establish a police force in London, with "prevention of crime" as its main function. This was approved by Parliament, and the Metropolitan Police Act was passed. The Act established the policing area and the Metropolitan Police District, and authorized the appointment of a Commander-in-Chief of the Metropolitan Police with the approval of the Home Secretary. The Act created the Metropolitan Police Office, which was responsible for investigating criminal activity and bringing suspects to account for their actions. The first Metropolitan Police officers began work on 29 September 1829, and from that date, the Metropolitan Police Service has been recognized as the world's first modern and professional police force. The principles developed by Sir Robert Peel have remained an important part of modern-day policing. To maintain public respect and support, the public must secure the willing cooperation of the public in voluntary observance of the law and must secure the public's respect and approval of our existence.

Also, safeguarding the public's trust and confidence in the police force in the United Kingdom is vital for a secure and long-lasting advantage. A victim of crime who knows that the officers are from the local police force and has seen them doing their best will gain confidence in the area and know that their quality of life will improve. Officers starting patrol on foot and getting to know residents and business owners will gain a greater understanding of the problems in that area and build more confidence in dealing with everyday situations. Local communities value police work and build better relationships, as they can tell who to approach when they need help or advice. Local police can receive more accurate support and help in solving problems if a similar approach is used. In general, greater support and good relations with local communities mean the police force can function more effectively. Now, his ideas and the Metropolitan Police model have been emulated and adopted in the USA and around the world. These mission statements and principles are built into law in the Police Act 1996 and the Police Reform Act 2002, and they underpin the work of every police force in England and Wales. That is to say, they set the standards by which the police must work to achieve the principles that Sir Robert Peel and the first Metropolitan Commissioner, Richard Mayne, set out over 180 years ago.

Influence of Colonialism on Policing Models

During the colonial era, administrators in many parts of the world established professional police forces to support new colonial governments and maintain law and order in the colonized territories. Policing models adopted during the colonial era were largely based on those of the colonial powers. Sir Robert Peel's Metropolitan Police Force in London was established in 1829 and is widely regarded as the world's first modern, professional police force. With the colonization of other parts of the world by European powers, including Britain, France, Portugal, and Holland, these colonial powers often developed police forces in their colonies that were similar in structure and organization to the Metropolitan Police in London. The "Metropolitan Police Model" was commonly adopted and introduced in many parts of the world during the colonial period. This is characterized by a professional, full-time, paid police force with a hierarchical, bureaucratic structure, a formal training academy, a clear, uniformed presence in public, and an organized, centralized detective unit. In turn, this policing model involves developing and maintaining a particular professional identity among police officers, such as providing social services to the public and ensuring public order, which becomes an essential police strategy and routine that lasts for decades. As a result, the belief and practice of professional or expert-oriented police forces have greatly influenced present-day police strategies and the development of modern policing models in many countries that have experienced a long history of colonialism. Such influence of colonial residues in the contemporary era can be observed in the continued emphasis on a professional police approach, as reflected in many traditional models of policing: the professional model, the community model, and the legalistic model.

Traditional Models of Policing

Reactive policing (RP) is a traditional model of policing, used when police resources are called into action. It is a time-consuming model of policing because it begins with the police waiting for the crime to occur. In RP, it is considered standard practice for police to respond to and arrest suspects after the offence. Moreover, the police do not take action until the crime is reported to them, thereby hindering efforts to deter crime proactively. On the other hand, proactive policing (PP) is a model of policing in which action is taken to prevent crime. It is an alternative to reactive policing, as it is considered a more intelligent and possibly successful model of policing. In PP, the police are proactive in seeking and arresting suspects before the crime is committed. However, for the police to be proactively involved in seeking and arresting suspects, they must demonstrate reasonable suspicion that someone is about to or will commit an offence. That gives the police significant power to stop individuals on the street to conduct searches or request information. Community-oriented policing (COP) is a local and decentralized approach to preventing crime. It aims to both reduce the fear of crime and enhance the quality of life within the community. COP is a partnership between the police and the local community to share responsibility for identifying and solving problems that can lead to crime. It builds better relationships with external partners and focuses on specific services for that community. Adopted from the United States, problem-oriented policing (POP) is a method used by police to identify what may lead to or contribute to criminal activity.

Reactive Policing

Reactive policing is the traditional model of policing most familiar to the general public. It is the standard mode of conventional law enforcement in which authorities respond to criminal incidents and citizens' calls for emergency via the deployment of police units. In reactive policing, it is the responsibility of police officers to take action when a crime has already been committed. The main focus of reactive policing is to conduct investigations of the crimes that have already occurred. Moreover, reactive policing is focused on random motorized patrols conducted by police officers. The seemingly undirected, untargeted activities of patrolling have been praised for their potential to prevent crime. However, these activities emanate from the traditionally reactive role of police officers, who are expected to respond to calls for service and to take action after a crime has been committed. According to the US Department of Justice, the development of computer-based information and telecommunications technology has challenged the traditional reactive policing model and has laid the foundations for police adopting a proactive model of policing. Several studies have found that reactive policing should be a small part of an overall police agency's strategic policing activities.

Proactive Policing

In proactive policing, the officers are trying to catch somebody. This is also sometimes known as a 'hunter' style of policing, which is fundamentally the opposite of reactive policing. Proactive policing follows a completely different approach to the philosophy of a reactive style of patrol. It differs even further, as it is a strategy with a much more intentional, planned approach. Teams or individual officers will gather information about criminal activity within their area. For example, they may notice a pattern in a certain area for burglaries. The officers may then decide to set up a police stakeout or an operation which is designed to catch the suspected criminals. Such an approach actually dates far back to the reform era of Sir Robert Peel. He introduced the first form of proactive policing when he established the Metropolitan Police in London in 1829. He introduced the patrol-based ideology, with police officers constantly circulating throughout their shift. This is a clear intention: to deter criminals from committing crimes in public view and, if a crime were to occur, to have an officer in the vicinity. Nowadays, new proactive policing strategies have been developed and introduced to aid the fight against crime in our communities. The intelligence-led, proactive policing style has become a model for many police forces around the world. This is where officers analyze and review patterns of crime and criminal behavior and use this information to schedule patrols and police time more effectively. By doing this, not only will it increase the chance of catching criminals, but it will also minimize the opportunity for them to commit crimes. By adopting modern, innovative methods of proactive policing, this has also boosted interest in this style of policing. Political figures and policing bodies have invested heavily in research and technology towards aiding the proactive fight against crime. However, with the key focus on such strategies, the downside is that reactive policing can sometimes be neglected, potentially leading to a rise in criminal activity that may go unnoticed. Therefore, it is vital to strike a balance between the two styles of police patrol work to ensure comprehensive public safety coverage. Both proactive and reactive styles of policing are, as a rule, a constant battle between the advancement of criminal activity and the evolution of investigative strategies and technology. With the introduction of body-worn cameras and mobile data terminals in police vehicles, officers can securely store and track significant evidence from crime scenes or incidents, while providing fast access to data for their colleagues. Such advancements are attempting to bolster a more mindful approach to proactive and preventive policing, instead of just relying on the 'point and shoot' methods of surveillance when an incident occurs. Nonetheless, it is predicted that technology will only advance further to help current and future police officers to protect and serve their communities.

Community-Oriented Policing

Community-oriented policing (COP) is a pattern of policing that brings police officers more into the public eye and police work into the public domain. It broadens the focus of fighting crime to include solving community problems and "manifestations of physical and social disorder". The main goal of COP is not to meet the traditional view of police work - as the criminal "rule of law" - but to promote a happier, less threatening and more prosperous community. It is based on the philosophy that the quality of life in the community can be improved and social disorder reduced through a partnership with the community, in which police respond to the community's concerns. There are three core components to COP.

They are: community partnership, organizational transformation, and problem-solving. The community partnership moves from the traditional policing of "us v them" (i.e. Police v the community) and invites the community to become part of the solution to its own problems. This can improve relations between the police and the public. By making people feel safer and more involved in the community, crime and social disorder can be reduced. The second core concept is organizational transformation. Police organizations that practice COP may be required to undergo a fundamental transformation from an autocratic and centralized form of police administration to one that is more "decentralized, participative, and based on a new value system that fosters a problem-solving and entrepreneurial approach" to police work. This means that many police officers - often those who have served for many years - will find themselves spending more time out of the office and on the street, working closely with the community. Thirdly, there is the requirement that officers practice problem-solving. This means that traditional methods of reacting quickly to unpredictable situations and of working only with other officers of the criminal justice system must be replaced by a broad, innovative, and effective approach to policing. Community-oriented policing advocates argue that by identifying the underlying causes of incidents, problems can be eradicated, and both the community and police can move away from the need for highly visible, intrusive measures such as arrests and/or court orders. For example, finding that an area suffers from heavy vandalism only at certain times of night can allow the police to direct resources more effectively by ensuring that there is a highly visible, quick, and decisive response for this period only. This kind of approach will be more effective and less damaging to police-community relations than a full-time curfew and the mass arrest of any youths found in the area during these times.

Problem-Oriented Policing

Traditional models of policing are based on the idea that police respond to serious criminal offences in a timely manner. The problems with this model are obvious - it is not effective at preventing crimes from occurring. Moreover, the police are not in a position to maintain order in public places and the community, which may lead to increased crime and a decline in residents' quality of life. Reactive policing is also called the "traditional" model of policing. This is the most widely used form of policing in the United States, although it is not the most effective. Under this model, the police focus on investigating crimes that have already taken place. They wait for crimes to be committed, and then they respond. In his essay *Problem-Oriented Policing*, Herman Goldstein criticizes reactive approaches in modern policing. He argues that the police should shift their focus from incidents to the underlying problems that cause them. With the traditional approach, the same criminal problems are likely to continue. Each incident is dealt with as a separate event, and the underlying problems that cause the incidents are not addressed. Goldstein is asking the police to make a basic shift in their work. Instead of simply reacting to crimes as they occur and trying to solve them through investigation, they should take the initiative to identify the problems and develop a strategy that focuses on them, not the incidents. The strategy would involve addressing the immediate problems and recommending long-term changes to the underlying problems that prevent crime. Goldstein's idea of problem-oriented policing represents a shift from "reactive" to "proactive" policing, in which police seek to address the fundamental conditions that give rise to crime. He challenges the effectiveness of simply increasing the arrest rates. Each time Keith and Reeves responded to a call, they felt they were playing a random game of "Whack a Mole". The reactive approach left both the officers and the citizens feeling as if they were not in control of the situation. With problem-oriented policing, we shift the focus to what happens before the crime rather than the crime itself. When the police examine the underlying problems that give rise to crime and develop strategies to prevent them, they can truly help society. Many police departments have adopted this new philosophy. Goldstein uses the term "problem-oriented policing" to describe a new way of thinking about police work. He describes it as "...a process and method of policing that identifies and recognizes specific problems which prompt the planning and implementing of carefully controlled and evaluated pendency of all realistic measures of dealing with them." He continues, "Problems come from many different sources and thus it will be necessary to distinguish problems that are the principle focus of the police activity from problems with other foci." Essentially, Goldstein is arguing for the police to change from the reactive, random, short-term-oriented philosophy of policing that adopts a crime-by-crime basis. Instead, he wants the police to play a more effective and efficient role in identifying the causes of incidents in time and reducing the number of such incidents. The main goals behind problem-oriented policing are:

- Reducing crime and improving the quality of life.
- Shaping a service that works together with the community and its strategic and practical problem-solving.

This approach will lead to more satisfied communities and police officers.

Contemporary Models of Policing

Intelligence-led policing involves collecting and analyzing information to guide police operations aimed at controlling crime and improving public safety. In intelligence-led policing, data collection and crime analysis are the most important components. The main goal is to produce timely and high-quality analysis to inform operational decision-making. Predictive policing is closely linked to the development of information technology and the widespread use of computerized crime mapping in policing. Predictive policing emphasizes the use of statistical analysis to identify the existence of crime series and patterns. The near-repeat phenomenon posits that when a crime occurs at a location, subsequent crimes in the following days are likely to occur near the same location. This phenomenon is the basis of predictive policing. Evidence-based policing is an approach to policy-making and tactical decision-making for police departments. It is influenced by the fields of criminology and criminal justice and involves the use of the best available research and evidence when making decisions. The evidence-based approach to policing is recognized as an effective strategy for measuring police operations and practices. It is intended to promote effective crime-control strategies, reduce unwarranted practice variations across the police department, and increase cost efficiency. Additionally, it encourages better and more effective relations with various units within police departments and other criminal justice agencies.

Intelligence-Led Policing

Intelligence-led policing (ILP) is a policing model that is built around the assessment and management of risk. In an ILP system, data analysis and criminal intelligence are used to inform and target proactive policing activities. By examining the output of the analysis, the police are able to make informed decisions about where they should focus their efforts. Furthermore, assessing risk within an ILP framework can take on different forms. For example, risk can be assessed by examining the threat a criminal poses to the public or by understanding the potential harm from a particular criminal act. Various risk assessment models are used in ILP. Parnaby proposes a typology (classification by general type) consisting of three types of information widely used by the police in different situations: general risk, specific risk, and incident assessment (Parnaby, 2010). Pope et al. describe a two-stage process: first, determining the likelihood of an incident, and then, if it were to occur, its severity, to provide a structured and auditable approach (Pope et al., 2000).

The concept of ILP began to gain currency in the late 1990s. Since that time, ILP has been implemented in a number of Western police forces, including the UK, the USA and Canada. However, as Scott points out, the concept has yet to be adequately theorized and needs to be articulated more clearly (Scott, 2008). It is worth noting that ILP is used within the UK National Intelligence Model, enabling the police to effectively manage the risk posed by all types of offences. Juan Du Barry defines the National Intelligence Model. According to him, the National Intelligence Model (NIM) provides the concepts and processes of intelligence-led policing in a structured and coherent manner that operates from the national to the local levels (Du Barry, 2006). He further argues that NIM is not simply an initiative but a program which aims to improve the management and application of knowledge.

Predictive Policing

Predictive policing is the use of mathematical, computer algorithms, and data analysis methods to identify and connect, or predict, possible criminal activity. Modern predictive policing is the most commonly recognized and robotic policing practice that has been implemented by many law enforcement agencies, and it represents investigated methods for future development in a better understanding of crime and in methods used to minimize local and international criminal issues. This kind of modern methodology is underpinned by two agreements. First and foremost, it is based on the understanding that it is possible to predict criminal activity, especially the spatially concentrated crime, and that police resources can be efficiently and effectively directed towards those forecasts. Predictive policing suggests that law enforcement agencies can use historical and current crime data to predict future crimes. 'PredPol' is a typical example of geographical predictive policing methodology that originated in Los Angeles, and it is a modern, patented criminal algorithm that works well to reduce future crime and is based on predictions of where and when crime is more likely to occur. PredPol can provide dynamic forecasts for multiple types of crime, including burglary, robbery, and vehicle theft. The command and control of every crime will be changed by applying PredPol's results, ensuring it makes human and modern connections to create and analyze citizens' everyday success. This modern predictive policing deepened its roots in criminal intelligence history in the mid-1990s. It will largely exclude criminal intelligence analysis from serious studies. It is to be widely untutored, but predictably it determines. The modern type of policing, called 'intelligence-led', is what most want to highlight as the modern methodologies. Such modern methodologies from the field are not focused on reactive practices, but rather on preventive approaches, and the leads that can be obtained from criminal analysis.

Evidence-Based Policing

There are some key concepts that constitute the basis of contemporary policing strategies. These are also the tools and methods used in evidence-based policing. For example, "hot spots," "repeat victimization," "space time clusters," "series and pattern analysis", and "forecasting" are now the commonly accepted terms and they are used as the key concepts of evidence-based policing in contemporary research or studies. When police leaders talk about implementing an evidence-based practice, they often refer to changing current hunches and unsupported beliefs about police work by using the latest scientific research. By using the statistics and research methods, police are now moving from the traditional professional model of policing to the knowledge-based, managerial form of evidence-based policing. It involves making decisions and formulating policies based on scientific evidence. The information and findings from studies that test the effectiveness of police tactics in controlling crime are now becoming the proper tools in police decision-making. For example, studies like the Minneapolis Domestic Violence Experiment, which was the first experiment on testing the effectiveness of arrest, demonstrated that arrest was more effective than any victim services or mediations in controlling domestic violence. Thanks to advances in methodological development in policing-related research, there is now a greater understanding of the importance of methodological procedures, such as sampling, measurement, design, and analysis, for drawing valid and convincing conclusions. Therefore, the experimentation and wide-ranging validation of the effectiveness of various tactics make evidence-based policing a desirable development for maintaining high-quality, effective police services. In recent years, there has been a profound shift in how law is understood.

Comparative Analysis of Policing Models

Enforcement and policing have been witnessed. Instead of weighing the kinds of policing strategies available to law enforcement or the concept of Intelligence-Led Policing (ILP), the field has evolved. Expert writers have begun to inquire about how "innovations and technology in the information-centric field" can be valuable for strategy typhoon and real-time adaptations of that method. Predicate policing claims that the police department can reduce future crimes, particularly by recognizing crime series, and analyzing a large combination of data in the historical crime briefings. Shift analysis in traditional patrolling strategies, regarding ILP, shows that patrolling resources would be temporarily removed from "other time periods with criminally slight" present crime series to give rise to crime effects. In delay-oriented policing, resources are employed to prevent crime from occurring, and it focuses on immediate, patrol-intensive controls. The most noteworthy limitation of this point of view is that we are sacrificing safety and strengthening the protection of residents and regulatory support when we use resources to stop crime effectively. However, in community patrolling, the study found that the police department placed about 85% or more of "resourced patrols" in non-residential areas, such as motor housing complexes, exchange parking lots, and other areas.

Strengths and Weaknesses of Traditional Models

Traditional models of policing focus on traditional law enforcement, such as patrol and criminal investigation. Firstly, the strength of this approach is that most police department structures are centralized, meaning resources are located in a single main area. Also, it appears that modern policing is about providing services to communities and neighborhoods through officers who are more proactive and interact with residents to solve their problems. However, the weaknesses of a traditional approach might confirm that it leads to a reactive style of law enforcement: the police act or make their presence known only when a crime has already been committed, a turnaround from the philosophy of community policing, which is based on prevention. Secondly, a reactive approach is consistent with the use of random motorized patrol as the primary patrol tactic or watch squad in workplaces, where police officers are assigned to survey geographic areas or specific buildings, such as shopping malls and schools, for criminal activity, fires, or hazards. However, random patrols are infrequently used, and their effectiveness is in question. In support of this argument, the Kansas City preventive patrol experiment was conducted, and it has been found that traditional motorized patrol has little or no impact on crime. Lastly, the evidence on the effectiveness of criminal investigation and arrest in crime prevention is promising, though not entirely persuasive. While to have a successful criminal investigation, police need to gather sufficient and admissible evidence to present in front of the courts, it is argued that for the most part, the solvability of most cases is relatively small, which means the higher the rate of "no suspect identified," the less effective this criminal investigation approach is.

Advantages and Limitations of Contemporary Models

First and foremost, contemporary policing has evolved over the years due to the major issues of increasing crime complexity and technological advances. Different models have provided new and revolutionary approaches in the law enforcement and policing system. Intelligence-led policing, also known as knowledge- or information-based policing, is a proactive, problem-solving approach to policing that uses the analysis of intelligence and crime data to prevent and reduce crime and improve the quality of life. The advantages of intelligence-led policing are as follows: it targets serious offenses, it targets prolific or serious offenders, it focuses on police resources based on intelligence received, it supports crime reduction through the development of effective strategies, it assists in the deployment of resources and facilitates the improved management of the demand for police services and police officers. On the limitations side, intelligence-led policing requires strong leadership and strategic vision. The shift from traditional policing to intelligence-led policing can be challenging due to established cultures and practices within the police service.

Furthermore, while it is important to acknowledge that most intelligence-led operations and other policing strategies are subject to some level of scrutiny and oversight, this is a significant issue due to the potential for abuse of police powers. Also, predictive policing is the use of analytical techniques. Advantages of predictive policing include, but are not limited to: it allows law enforcement agencies to make use of the limited resources they have to the maximum, it targets crime which can lead to significant harm to vulnerable victims, it can be used to support evidence-based decision making on issues of potential harm, it can be used to support resources being made available to work to prevent the identified crime. On the limitations side, predictive policing, like other models, is most effectively undertaken when collaboration among police and other community stakeholders is established, including local authorities, health bodies, housing and probation services, and even the general public. As an emerging field, common standards, methodologies, and expertise among police, technology, and civilian-trained analysts do not yet exist. The successful implementation of predictive policing strategies depends on the credibility of the theories used to explain and predict the spatial and temporal distributions of crime, and the extent to which practitioners believe in these theories. Cultures in police agencies can, therefore, be defined as a form of learned behavior that is shared by members and should be introduced centrally, but in some organizations, a "just do it" form of policing can be prevalent, therefore creating a climate of using intuitions and previous experience as opposed to crime data. Cultures can be a significant challenge to implementing a data-driven strategy because people are often resistant to change. But research has shown that culture change can be managed and achieved if top-level police management actively promotes and encourages intelligence-based working, openly endorses and supports new systems, processes, and organizational restructuring, and provides reassurance to staff through in-depth partnership working and helping to create a realization and awareness of the benefits that can be achieved.

Implementing Effective Policing Strategies

For policing leaders and administrators, it is important to understand how to effectively implement modern changes and strategies. Over the past three decades, the nation's police leaders have been led to believe that the use of popular new management methods and technologies, along with a focus on the "business" of policing, will produce significant organizational change. Unfortunately, only limited evidence suggests that many contemporary police management strategies have produced positive results in achieving effective organizational change. The scholars distinguish management from leadership. They argue that while management focuses on the status quo, leadership is primarily about change and adaptation. To date, the leaders of the nation's police organizations have focused more on management practices to make organizations more efficient and predictable, rather than on leadership practices that can produce more adaptive and meaningful change within the organization and in its service to the community. These research findings have important implications for the socialization and training of the new generation of police leaders. More leadership and less management training needs to be developed for those who aspire to the rank of chief and are already well established at higher levels within the organization. In addition, it is critical that formal police leadership is embedded within higher education and becomes a fundamental part of effective, principled police organizations, rather than focusing solely on specialized training for those already in higher ranks. In many urban police organizations, the community's perceived demand for greater accountability on the part of the police, as well as the increases in technological capabilities for data collection and analysis, has driven and legitimized the use of both qualitative and quantitative measures of police performance. Such measures span the gamut of activities in which the police engage, from the number of arrests and citizen complaints, to response times and hourly patrol checks. However, the onerous reality of adopting a management objective that focuses on the use of performance measures as a means for shaping behavior and optimizing results is that it can become a powerful and sometimes single focus of assessment - a pitfall to which contemporary police leaders have succumbed. Yet such practices typically fail to capture the importance of the variety of ways in which police can demonstrate responsive, proactive, and morally informed obligations to address and prevent criminal behavior of all types.

Specifically, that means fostering a climate within the organization that formally recognizes leaders and leadership actions; recognizes moments when officers take charge of difficult social and criminal situations; recognizes when officers call upon community resources and input to help create mutual and collective solutions to crime; and tracks and celebrates the myriad ways officers serve and engage their communities, such as coaching, mentoring, and working to create and support community events and projects. Such a climate will be marked by the recognition of interdependent and contingent acts of leadership and the creation of new pathways for achieving adaptive change.

Conclusion & Suggestions

Based on an analysis of police systems across countries, the following suggestions are made:

- There is a need to amend the various Police Acts in the country to enhance accountability and transparency in police operations.
- Instead of governmental functionaries, independent personnel with wide experience and knowledge in law, management, accounting, social services, etc., should be appointed as members of the bodies that make appointments and handle complaints against police.

As pointed out in the Prakash Singh judgment, there should be an independent Police Complaints Authority to handle complaints against police men and an independent State Security Commission to handle the appointment of top officials of the police.

The members of these bodies should be selected through an open recruitment process, and the selection committee may comprise members currently listed on the State Security Commission. At least 1/3rd of the members of the State Security commission and Police Complaints Authority shall be drawn from the judiciary/legal academicians in consultation with the Chief Justice of the High Court.

The functions of the State Security Commission should also include general supervision of investigative functions, including providing facilities for crime investigation, though it is not desirable to give the Commission any powers to interfere in case-to-case investigation. The State Security Commission, as envisaged in the draft National Police Commission, is also an appellate authority to which complaints regarding illegal or irregular orders from superiors are to be made. A proper avenue for venting such complaints and, more importantly, for recording them would foster a sense of independence in the police psyche, which is essential to ensuring a free and fearless police force. The Police Complaints Authority should be given the power to record all sorts of complaints against police officers and to publish the details thereof on its website for public scrutiny. This would help ensure greater accountability in the police. There should be a proper enforcement mechanism for the findings of the Police Complaints Authority. The findings of the Authority should be final, and the Police Complaints Authority should be designated as the sole disciplinary authority over the police officials; failing in the exercise of the Police Complaints Authority in the discharge of their duties would go to waste.

In conclusion, it must be said that if policing in India is to imbibe the true spirit of community participation and become a role model for policing, then the emphasis on executive discretion should give way to participatory policing, and its administration should be made more transparent and participatory. It should be borne in mind that, in a modern democracy, the police play a significant role in maintaining the social fabric and ensuring the continuance of democracy. Hence, it is important to modify the negative perception about the police that is deeply rooted in the common people's psyche as an instrument of torture by the power wielders, and to create a feeling of comity in the public mind that the police are their friend and guide and their representative in combating crime. They are accountable to the public for their deeds and misdeeds. Equally important is the feeling of comfort in the minds of police men who should be freed from arbitrary interference from powers-that-be in the discharge of their duties to ensure their allegiance to the cause of common people and to uphold the scepter of justice entrusted to them by law in a just and equitable manner, acceptable to common people.

Summary

How easily can democratic policing replace authoritarian policing? Is it possible to adapt the concept of community policing to local environments in developing countries? The case studies in this paper from the Vera Institute of Justice suggest that efforts to introduce community policing often run into serious difficulties, hindered by low levels of professionalism within police agencies, public disrespect for law enforcement, and a lack of community organization. The case studies also suggest that there is no single ideal uniform model for community policing, as both local context and history are highly influential on success.

Countries in the developing world have sought to adopt community policing to make police more accountable to their citizens. However, community policing was developed in Western democracies under very different conditions from those in these countries. The case studies show how the concept has been adapted in Brazil, Haiti, Uganda and South Africa. The likelihood of structural reform was highest in countries with strong support for the initiative and extensive grassroots community organizations. In situations with little support from top police officers, little grassroots support, police agencies with inadequate resources, corruption problems and/or lack of public goodwill, there will be significant problems. In these situations, community policing is likely to be an isolated effort, limited to a few demonstration sites (for example, Brazil) or to small groups of officials while the rest of the police force goes on with business as usual (for example, Uganda and Haiti).

In Brazil, which is regarded as a relative success, NGOs and foreign governments played a key role in initiating and supporting community-policing efforts. In Western democracies, implementations often fall short of expectations and significant change in community perceptions of the police, fear of crime and crime rates are unusual. In developing countries with meagre funds and built on shaky police, community relations do not always persist. The Western community-policing model aims to achieve a handful of goals, primarily by improving police-community relations and implementing strategic structural changes within police organizations, such as decentralizing authority and encouraging public participation. In the case studies and sites considered, they were only partially moving towards these ends. Other points to consider:

Countries coping with histories marred by brutality, violence and corruption will have social environments that are hostile to policing. Community policing programs should involve genuine effort toward reform.

Neighborhood patrols can help promote social control rather than dynamically transforming the community-police relationship.

Input from foreign governments and NGOs can be crucial in situations like Brazil, where decentralization led to experimentation with different models and advanced technologies, thereby enhancing accountability and transparency.

Raising expectations without genuine reform is likely to deepen the rift between the citizens and the police.

Lessons Learned from Comparative Study

An analysis of various models brings out the following lessons:

- Popular consent in policing is a highly uncertain concept, and policing by law and by consent is now almost intertwined.
- Most countries, regardless of the model they follow, place importance on public consultations and local support in policing activities, though sometimes not formally.

In almost all these sample jurisdictions, except China, there is a clear separation of crime investigation from law-and-order maintenance duties.

Lessons from the Developmental History of the Indian Police Structure

At this juncture, it is pertinent to examine the ancient system of policing prevalent in India. A vivid picture of the ancient police system is available in various ancient texts, including *the Arthasastra* by Kautilya (Chanakya). The ancient police system in India was based on the principle of local responsibility and mutual cooperation. In the village, security and peace were a matter of collective responsibility, shared by every resident. One of the villagers, called the gramneta or village watchman, was responsible for protecting the village from the criminals. In contrast, the body corporate of the village was bound to make good the loss due to crime committed within the village limits, except in cases where they were able to trace the offenders or fix responsibility for the crime upon neighboring villages. [11] This village level responsibility continues, though in its rudiments, even today, which is seen embodied in section 40 of Code of Criminal Procedure, 1973, which imposed a duty on officers employed in connection with the affairs of a village and each person residing in a village to communicate to the nearest magistrate or to the officer in charge of the nearest police station certain information.

Police commission of 1860, whose recommendations culminated in the Indian Police Act, 1861, recommended that Police under each local government or administration shall constitute one force and be under the officer to be styled Inspector General of Police, in whom should be vested the control over the organization, the responsibility of maintaining it in a state of efficiency by proper attention to its training and discipline, internal economy and its general rearrangement through its own officers. It was also inter alia recommended that the office of the village watchman should be retained, being an ancient institution of India, since the village watchman was "a man of the village but not enough an official to be alien or obnoxious to the villagers, but only an official to be amenable to systems and reliable for duty on behalf of the police."

Thus, it can be seen that the British, however contemptuous they were of the integrity of local people, were convinced that policing would not be successful without a tolerably reliable agency in the villages. The Indian Police Act, 1861, did not come into force automatically in all the provinces, as it contained a provision stating that the Act would apply to any province only when so notified by the Governor General in Council. The Act was never applied in the provinces of Madras, Bombay, and Sind, which had separate Police Acts (the Police Act of 1859 in Madras and the Bombay District Police Act II of 1867 in Bombay were almost identical to the Indian Police Act, 1861, with certain changes based on local conditions). The Police Commission of 1902 recommended establishing a separate Criminal Investigation Department in each province to collect and disseminate information on criminals and organized crime, and to assist in the investigation of complex cases. It also recommended establishing an organization under the Inspector General of Police for the whole of India, in the line of the Police Organization for Provinces. It also contained an important recommendation outlining the paramount importance of developing and fostering the existing village agency for police work. A comparative study of the policing across the models examined, undertaken by Nation Master [14], shows that of the models examined, the percentage rate of public confidence in policing is as follows: The United Kingdom: 77%, the USA: 73%, France: 67. The other countries, including India, are not even featuring in the sampling. This can give rise to an assumption that multiple police forces instil more confidence in the public about the policing, as they have more reach than a singular system, as followed in Saudi Arabia or China, but this conclusion should be taken only with caution, as the sampling may not even have included these countries.

Assimilation of Lessons

As a democracy, India should be striving towards an inclusive policing, where policing functions are carried out with popular consent, and accountability and transparency are also required. In this, the British model of making police accountable to the public is worth emulating. In fact, the Police Complaints Authority (PCA), which has already been brought into force in many states in India as a result of the Prakash Singh judgment [15], is nothing but a copy of the English model. While the UK model emphasizes participatory management of the police system, the Indian models appear to emphasize vesting greater discretion in executive authorities. It is also sad to note that the existing reform recommendations [16] offer no suggestions to augment the village-level policing system. S 72 of the draft Kerala Police Act, 2008, for example, provides for a system of community policing, which is perhaps the sole proposition in the whole draft statute that calls for community consultations. However, there are no provisions that make the recommendations of the Community Liaison Group mandatory, which would make community policing an exercise in creating informants rather than participants in the policing process. Even the Police Commissions appointed by successive governments, which served as the basis for the Supreme Court's guidelines in this regard, did not place greater emphasis on democratization than on the independence of the police force from governmental intervention.

Chapter 7 | MANAGERIAL AND ORGANIZATIONAL CHALLENGES

Mark Moore, Mark Moore

Introduction

In their influential work on policing and public management, particularly regarding the transition from the traditional "reform era" model to community- and problem-oriented policing, Mark Moore and John Eck identified several key managerial and organizational challenges. These challenges often centered on moving police departments away from a rigid, centralized, incident-driven approach towards a more flexible, decentralized, and proactive one. The primary challenges include:

A fundamental shift from traditional output measures (arrests, response times, clearance rates) to a broader definition of success based on outcomes, such as reduced crime and disorder, increased public safety, and improved community satisfaction.

Overcoming the deeply ingrained "police culture" that often resisted innovation and new strategies was a significant hurdle.

This culture was often preoccupied with an "us vs them" mentality and standard, reactive operating procedures. Concerns were raised that new policing strategies, such as community engagement and problem-solving, would distract police from their core responsibilities of crime prevention and law enforcement. The traditional model relied on centralized, command-and-control management to ensure compliance and prevent corruption. The new strategies required a degree of decentralization to empower field officers to make decisions and build community relationships, which created tension with existing hierarchies. Existing work rules and elaborate disciplinary procedures, often solidified by police unions, were seen as inhibiting strategic innovation and effective management of officer performance. Implementing new strategies, such as problem-oriented policing (POP), required better systems for gathering, analyzing, and using data at a local level (e.g., the SARA model), which challenged existing information systems and communication practices. A shift in strategy required new leadership skills, moving from rigid, top-down command to more facilitative leadership that could guide and empower officers to use imagination and creativity to solve problems. Bringing police into closer contact with partisan and community political pressures raised fears of "re-politicizing" the police force, which the reform era had sought to avoid. Limited financial resources and inherent uncertainties regarding the effectiveness of new approaches often discouraged innovation and comprehensive implementation. Moore and Eck argued that these challenges needed to be addressed strategically for police departments to effectively evolve their mission and operations to meet contemporary public safety needs and implement the administrative changes required for community policing, moving from a hierarchical command structure to a more decentralized, empowering model.

Managerial Challenges

Mark Moore and John Eck's work, particularly in the context of policing and public management, identified several key managerial and organizational challenges arising from traditional hierarchical and bureaucratic structures. Their analysis helped drive the shift toward community and problem-oriented policing models, highlighting the following challenge: defining what constituted effective policing beyond traditional, easily measurable metrics such as arrest numbers or response times. They argued managers needed to define a broader mission centered on "creating public value" and then be held accountable for achieving these more complex, often qualitative, outcomes. Traditional police bureaucracy often discouraged individual initiative and problem-solving among lower-ranked officers. Moore and Eck stressed the need for management to empower frontline officers to analyze and address underlying community problems, rather than just reacting to individual incidents as they occurred. They noted a tendency toward reactive, incident-driven policing (the "standard model"). Managers faced the challenge of shifting the organizational focus from a purely reactive stance to proactive, strategic planning aimed at preventing crime and improving community conditions. Training and motivating staff to adopt new, more collaborative approaches to policing (e.g., community engagement, problem-solving) was a significant managerial hurdle, as it required a fundamental change in mindset and skill sets.

Organizational Challenges

The rigid, top-down nature of police departments created inefficiencies and communication gaps, making it difficult to adapt quickly to new situations or community needs. The challenge was moving towards "post-bureaucratic forms of organization" that were more flexible and learning-oriented. Implementing new strategies, such as community- or problem-oriented policing, faced significant internal resistance due to established routines, an entrenched organizational culture, and a lack of buy-in across all levels of the hierarchy. The organizational structure often failed to facilitate the systematic collection and use of local information and community feedback for organizational learning and adaptation. Management needed to create systems for monitoring that induced learning, not just compliance. Addressing complex issues often requires collaboration with other government agencies and community groups. A key organizational challenge was overcoming histories of antagonism, mistrust, and different organizational goals to work effectively in partnership. In the era of political policing, the challenges were corruption and political interference. In later eras, the challenge became maintaining public trust and legitimacy by ensuring that police operations aligned with societal standards of fairness and accountability, which required transparent, lawful conduct.

Mark H. Moore, author of *Creating Public Value: Strategic Management in Government*, is the Daniel and Florence Guggenheim Professor of Criminal Justice Policy and Public Management, John F. Kennedy School of Government, Harvard University. Anthony A. Braga is Senior Research Associate in the Program in Criminal Justice Policy and Management of the Malcolm Wiener Center for Social Policy, John F. Kennedy School of Government, Harvard University. They have an idea of the kinds of deliberative processes that should, ideally, go into the formation of a collective judgment about the good and the right as they apply to public police departments. In short, the important question at the core of developing any adequate measure of police performance is for citizens and their elected representatives to decide what is intrinsically valuable, or what we as a political community value, in the activities and operations of a public police department. That is simultaneously an issue for political philosophy and practical politics, as well as for professional management and science.

Citizens have long wanted a reliable measure of police performance. They want to know whether the police are producing something that is valuable with the assets entrusted to them. They want to be able to hold the organization to account for its performance. Police managers, too, have needed a measure of police performance, partly to meet external demands for accountability and partly to establish accountability within their organizations, thereby focusing attention on achieving valuable results rather than simply on reliably executing established policies and procedures. A crucial task for both citizens and police managers, then, is to develop an understanding of how the "public value" produced by policing can be recognized and assessed. Generally speaking, developing appropriate measures of police performance has been treated as a managerial or technical problem to be solved through some combination of the practical methods of business management (develop a "bottom line" for policing) or the statistical methods of social science (conduct a "program evaluation" of police departments focusing on the ultimate outcomes produced by the police). And it is true, of course, that developing suitable performance measures does raise important managerial, technical, and scientific issues. The managerial issues focus on how different measurement systems can be used to guide, motivate, or enable the learning of an organization. The technical issues concern developing statistical measures and instruments that reliably capture the performance dimensions the police deem important. The scientific inquiry focuses on the extent to which performance measurement systems can help police determine which programs "work" to accomplish various police objectives.

In the end, though, it seems self-evident that the development of police performance measures is also, and perhaps most fundamentally, a normative and political question; not only or even primarily a management or technical issue. After all, to develop a standard for assessing the performance of an organization as "good" or "bad," "improving" or "deteriorating," is to make a normative, value claim as well as a positive, scientific claim. One has to have an idea of what is "good" or "right" as it applies to police operations to defend a standard of police performance. One also has to have a theory about whose views of the "good" and the "right" should count in setting a standard for policing-more particularly, whether it is the views of individuals deciding for themselves what they think is "good" and "right" as they encounter the police as individuals seeking assistance or individuals who are stopped, cited, or arrested; or whether the idea of the good and the right in policing emerge from some kind of collective political process in which the body politic gathers itself together to say what is good and right for the whole, and where that view trumps the views of individuals. One may also need to understand the kinds of deliberative processes that should, ideally, go into the formation of a collective judgment about the good and the right as they apply to public police departments. In short, the important question at the core of developing any adequate measure of police performance is for citizens and their elected representatives to decide what is intrinsically valuable, or what we as a political community value, in the activities and operations of a public police department. That is simultaneously an issue for political philosophy and practical politics, as well as for professional management and science. Indeed, once one sees the issue as a normative, philosophical, and political question, a great many additional questions arise, including the following: Who does the valuing of public sector operations? Are police operations properly evaluated by the "customers" of the police (those who receive services from the police and/or pay the costs of keeping the police operating)? Or, are the police properly evaluated against a collectively established understanding of the "mission" of the police that serves as an alternative standard for judging police performance, one that emphasizes a shared social judgment about what constitutes a good and right police department and trumps the views of individuals who might want something different from that social standard? If the latter is true, who is the "we" that gets to establish the social standard for good and just policing? How do we form an articulate "we" from the crowd of individuals that "we" are, and where should "we" go to seek guidance in our deliberations about what we should want in policing? Assuming for a minute that the appropriate arbiter of the value of police activities is the political collective, how should that political collective-that "we"-think about the fact that the police routinely use force and authority to accomplish their purposes? Should that "we" think of force and authority as a kind of resource that has instrumental value like money, or should we view it as something quite different from money? If it is like money, should we be interested in economizing on its use? If it differs from money, what does its use require of us? Should the "we" formed in these collective decision-making processes view the public police instrumentally, as an agency trying to accomplish a public good, such as reduced crime or enhanced security? Or, should we think of the police in more intrinsic, principled terms as an entity that is responsible for enforcing the law fairly and impartially, regardless of the practical results? Or, should we think of the police as a complex blend of an instrumental agency that has resources that are to be deployed efficiently or effectively to achieve a social purpose, but where the social purpose we seek is not just reduced crime, or enhanced security, but also the quality of justice as it exists and is experienced in our communities? What is the relationship between the decisions about whether to value in instrumental or non-instrumental terms on the one hand, and whether organizations should be evaluated in terms of outcomes or processes on the other? Are the important outcomes of policing reduced crime and enhanced security, or should we view the achievement of justice as an outcome that ought to be pursued?

Can we see the "quality of justice" as a valued outcome of organizational activity that can justify the use of money as well as a process value? Is achieving justice as important as a social goal, or less important, or more important than reducing crime or enhancing security?

Mark H. Moore

Mark H. Moore is the Research Professor of Public Management. His current primary focus is studying the processes that enable social innovation and change in response to changing political, economic, and social conditions.

He began his career at the Kennedy School as a member of the inaugural class of the master's program in public policy, and was subsequently awarded one of Harvard's first PhDs in public policy. After being appointed assistant professor in 1974, Moore took a two-year leave to serve as the chief planning officer at the newly created Drug Enforcement Agency. In 1978, he was appointed the first Guggenheim Professor of Criminal Justice Policy and Management, and used that position to launch the Kennedy School's Criminal Justice Program. At that time, he was also asked to lead the Kennedy School's "strategic management cluster," which was tasked with developing a distinctive approach to public management that could integrate the school's interests in policy analysis and improving government policy-making processes with the more traditional concerns of public administration. He was also appointed to chair the newly created Faculty Committee on Executive Programs through which the concepts being developed could be tested for utility and value with practising public executives. In 1998, Moore was appointed the Hauser Professor of Non-profit Organizations, and served as the first Faculty Director of the newly created Hauser Center for Non-profit Organizations. The aim of the Center was to focus Kennedy School attention on the important role of civil society actors in shaping government's (and therefore society's) overall capacity to identify, understand, and ameliorate pressing social problems. In 2007, he took up a half-time appointment as a professor at the Harvard Business School to learn how they thought about and taught social entrepreneurship and social enterprise. In 2008, he served in a half-time position as the Simon Professor of Organizations, Management, and Education at Harvard's Graduate School of Education to help that school design and launch a special program for educators, administrators, and social entrepreneurs seeking to close the "achievement gap" in American education.

In 2014, with the knowledge gained from time at both HBS and HGSE, Moore returned to the Kennedy School on a full-time basis to work on its Social Innovation and Change Initiative. The principal task was to further develop a course entitled "Sparking Social Change" that sought to enable students who came to the Kennedy School to imagine and pursue an idea for creating public value that could scale to significance from any particular position in society they might occupy – a task that continues today.

His publications are spread across three broad fields. In the field of public management, his works include: *Creating Public Value: Strategic Management in Government*; *Recognizing Public Value, and the Forthcoming Delivering Public Value: Operational Management in the Public Sector*. In the field of criminal justice, his works include: *Dangerous Offenders: The Elusive Targets of Justice*; *Beyond 9/11: A New Era for*

Policing; and *From Children to Citizens: The Mandate for Juvenile Justice*. In the field of social innovation, he is trying to catch up with the modern age and is developing digital materials to support the course on "Sparking Social Change." Moore holds a B.A. from Yale University (Summa Cum Laude and Honors with Exceptional Distinction in Political Science and Economics), and an M.P.P. and PhD from the Kennedy School of Government, Harvard University.

Mark Moore, a prominent expert in criminal justice policy and public management, is widely recognized for his substantial contributions to policing theory and practice, primarily through his advocacy for problem-oriented policing and the concept of "creating public value" in government.

- **Problem-Oriented Policing (POP):** Moore, in collaboration with others like George Kelling, challenged the traditional "professional strategy of policing" (which focused on rapid response to calls and routine patrol). He advocated that police departments shift from a reactive to a proactive, analytical approach, encouraging officers to identify and address underlying community problems that drive crime and disorder rather than just responding to incidents.
- **"Creating Public Value":** In his influential book *Creating Public Value: Strategic Management in Government*, Moore developed a framework for public sector leaders to focus their organizations on a clear mission, develop measurable goals, and embrace political accountability for achieving those goals. This concept applies directly to policing, urging police agencies to move beyond simply enforcing the law and fighting crime to actively producing public value by improving community safety and quality of life.
- **Community Policing and Strategy:** Moore's work has been instrumental in developing modern community policing models that emphasize collaborative partnerships between the police and the community. He argued that

police must seek broader consultation with citizens, take community input on priorities seriously, and use community surveys to evaluate effectiveness.

- **Performance Measurement:** He has written extensively on how to measure police performance effectively in this "new paradigm of policing". His work helps police departments develop measurement systems that guide, motivate, and enable learning within the organization, focusing not just on crime statistics but also on the quality of community relations and the effectiveness of problem-solving efforts. Moore was the Daniel and Florence Guggenheim Professor of Criminal Justice Policy and Management at the Harvard Kennedy School for many years, where he educated generations of police leaders and researchers. Mark H. Moore, a prominent expert in public policy and management, played a crucial role in developing the conceptual framework for community policing and problem-oriented policing. His contributions provided the intellectual foundation for a major shift in policing strategy away from traditional, reactive methods.
- **"Corporate Strategies for Policing":** In a seminal 1981 paper titled *Corporate Strategies for Policing*, co-authored with George Kelling,Moore argued that police should define their goals more broadly than just crime fighting and embrace strategies that involve the community. He emphasized that police work should address citizens' sense of security and fear of crime, not just official crime statistics. Defining "Public Value" in Policing, Moore conceptualized the core function of police as producing "public value." This goes beyond simply responding to incidents and includes improving community conditions, strengthening social institutions, and enhancing the overall quality of life.
- **Community Engagement as a Core Strategy:** He advocated for broad community consultation and

information-gathering to inform police priorities. This involves engaging citizens in face-to-face contact and incorporating community surveys into performance evaluations.

- **Problem-Solving Approach:** Moore's work laid the groundwork for integrating problem-solving techniques into standard police practice. Instead of only addressing incidents in isolation, he promoted identifying the root causes of recurring public safety issues and crafting tailored, often community-based, responses.
- **Challenging the Traditional Model:** He critically examined the classical bureaucratic model of policing, which often relied on centralized authority and impersonal relations, and advocated for more decentralized, community-oriented structures, such as neighborhood police stations. Moore's work provided the analytical tools and philosophical justification for law enforcement agencies to reorient their mission and operations toward building partnerships and proactively addressing community problems.

JohnE.Eck

John Eck is a highly influential figure in modern policing, known primarily for his work on problem-oriented policing (POP), the development of the SARA problem-solving model, and research on crime and place. Guides by this Author: *Student Party Riots (2006), Assessing Responses to Problems* (2002), *Understanding Risky Facilities (2007), Spectator Violence in Stadiums (2008), Pedestrian Injuries & Fatalities (2007), Street Robbery (2010), Home Invasion Robbery (2012), Monitoring Offenders on Conditional Release (2016).*

John Eck is a professor of criminal justice at the University of Cincinnati, where he teaches graduate courses in research methods, police effectiveness, crime policy, and crime prevention. He is the co-author, with Ronald V. Clarke, of *Becoming a Problem-Solving Crime Analyst.* From 1977 to 1994, he directed research at the

Police Executive Research Forum in Washington, D.C., where he conducted studies of criminal investigations management and drug markets, and helped to test and implement problem-oriented policing in agencies throughout the United States. From 1995 to 1998, Eck served as the evaluation coordinator for the Washington/Baltimore High-Intensity Drug Trafficking Area, where he developed methods to assess the effectiveness of drug trafficking enforcement. Eck has written extensively on problem-oriented policing, crime mapping, drug markets, computer simulation of crime patterns, and crime prevention. He was a member of the National Academy of Sciences Committee on Police Policy and Research and is a judge for the British Home Office's Tilley Award for Problem-Solving Excellence. Eck's research interests include the causes and prevention of crime and disorder, and the ways crime patterns develop and change. Eck received a master's degree in public policy from the University of Michigan in 1977 and a doctorate from the University of Maryland in 1994. John E. Eck is an Emeritus Professor of Criminal Justice at the University of Cincinnati, widely recognized for his expertise in crime prevention and problem-oriented policing. He has significantly influenced modern policing strategies through his research and publications.

- Career, Contributions and Academic Role: Eck taught graduate courses at the University of Cincinnati in areas such as research methods, crime policy, police effectiveness, and crime prevention.
- Police Executive Research Forum (PERF): He directed research at PERF from 1977 to 1994, managing studies and helping implement problem-oriented policing in police agencies.
- Key Research Areas:His work includes the causes and prevention of crime, crime patterns, crime mapping, and the effectiveness of police interventions. He is a leading scholar on problem-oriented policing.

- Publications: Eck has written many academic papers and co-authored *Becoming a Problem-Solving Crime Analyst* with Ronald V. Clarke.
- Awards and Recognition: He was part of the National Academy of Sciences Committee on Police Policy and Research. He received the Ronald V. Clarke Award and the Collaborative Agreement Award in 2016 for his work related to policing.
- Education PhD in Criminology: University of Maryland (1994). Note: Other notable individuals named John Eck include Johnny Eck (John Eckhardt Jr., 1911–1991), a sideshow performer and actor, and Johann Eck (1486–1543), a German theologian who opposed Martin Luther. This information pertains to the criminologist John E. Eck.
- Problem-Oriented Policing (POP) Implementation: Eck was a leading researcher at the Police Executive Research Forum (PERF), where he conducted studies and helped test and implement Herman Goldstein's concept of POP in agencies across the US. His work moved POP from a theoretical framework to a practical policing strategy.
- The SARA Model: In collaboration with William Spelman, Eck developed the SARA model, a structured, four-step process for police to address crime and disorder.
  - ✓ Scanning: Identifying recurring problems of concern to the community and the police.
  - ✓ Analysis: Systematically gathering information to identify the underlying causes of the problem. This phase often involves using the "crime triangle" to understand the relationship between victims, offenders, and places.
  - ✓ Response: Developing and implementing tailor-made solutions to address the root causes identified during the analysis phase.

- ✓ Assessment: Evaluating the impact of responses to determine whether the problem was reduced or eliminated, and making adjustments if necessary.

- Crime and Place Research (Hot Spots Policing): Eck's research focuses on the causes of high-crime locations ("hot spots") and on effective police interventions in those areas. His work emphasizes that crime is often concentrated in specific microgeographic areas and that policing efforts should be targeted to these areas to effectively control crime.
- Situational Crime Prevention and Place Management: He has written extensively on situational crime prevention, which focuses on altering the environment or conditions that enable crime. A key part of this is the concept of "place managers" (e.g., property owners, business managers) and how they can be engaged to prevent crime on their premises.
- Evidence-Based Policing: Throughout his academic career and extensive publications, Eck has been a strong advocate for evidence-based practices in policing, advocating rigorous research and evaluation to determine what actually works in crime prevention.

John Eck is a Professor Emeritus in the School of Criminal Justice at the University of Cincinnati and continues to influence police policy and research.

Mark Moore, Guggenheim Professor of Criminal Justice Policy and Management at Harvard, has written extensively about the fundamental managerial and organizational challenges facing police departments as they shift toward community- and problem-oriented policing. His work emphasizes that traditional police culture and structure often hinder effective strategic change.

Critical Comments on Managerial and Organizational Challenges

Moore's critical analysis of police management highlights several deep-seated issues. Moore, with co-authors such as David Kennedy, identified "inertial pressures" within traditional police culture that resist strategic management and organizational change. This culture, often focused on rapid response and crime fighting as the primary "real police work," devalues the proactive, community-engagement, and problem-solving aspects of modern policing. A significant challenge lies in measuring police performance beyond simple metrics like arrest numbers or response times. Moore argued that police agencies often struggle to define and measure the "public value" they create, making it difficult to drive the organization toward desired community outcomes and hold them accountable for achieving those purposes. Police organizations often lack the capacity for genuine strategic planning and long-term problem-solving, instead operating on a reactive, incident-by-incident basis. This inhibits their ability to address underlying community problems effectively. While community policing requires decentralizing authority to allow local officers to innovate and build community ties, police organizations often struggle with distributing decision-making authority effectively.

Concluding Comments

Moore's concluding thoughts stress that the transition to more effective policing models requires a profound shift in thinking: The fundamental challenge is philosophical as much as technical. Leaders must clarify the core values and purposes the organization should achieve, focusing on enhancing the "public good" and building legitimacy. Effective leadership is crucial to breaking down internal resistance and implementing necessary changes. Leaders must be able to manage for results in a complex environment where outcomes are often hard to quantify. Moore's work aligns with the idea that fair and transparent procedures are essential for building public trust, which in turn enhances police legitimacy and effectiveness.

Future Direction

For the future of policing, Moore advocated several strategic directions: future policing must adopt a result-oriented approach, using sophisticated measurement systems that capture community impact, safety, and legitimacy, rather than focusing solely on traditional outputs. The future involves moving beyond treating each call as a separate incident, instead identifying the underlying problems and collaborating with other government and community agencies to address them systemically. Police organizations need better mechanisms for storing and sharing knowledge, enabling continuous learning and adaptation to dynamic environments. Future police departments will need more flexible, agile, and outward-focused organizational structures that can adapt to a complex, digitalized, and transnational criminal landscape. Mark Moore's work provides a framework for understanding that effective policing is a strategic management challenge that demands ongoing innovation and a commitment to creating public value in collaboration with the communities they serve.

Part III
Evaluation, Challenges, and Future Directions

INTRODUCTION

The evaluation of community policing highlights positive effects on citizen satisfaction and police legitimacy but reveals limited effects on crime reduction and fear of crime. Key challenges include implementation inconsistencies and institutional resistance, while future directions involve greater integration with technology and community partners. Several key thinkers have shaped the discourse on community policing, including Robert C. Trojanowicz, who emphasized community policing as a long-term strategic approach based on partnership and accountability. James Q. Wilson identified different styles of policing (watchman, legalistic, service), which provided a framework for understanding the shift to community-oriented approaches. Herman Goldstein is associated with the Problem-Oriented Policing (POP) model, a foundational element of community policing that emphasizes identifying and solving underlying community problems rather than merely reacting to incidents. Malcolm Sparrow is a contemporary thinker who has written about the challenges of performance measurement in policing, particularly given the diverse nature of community problems.

Chapter 8 | ASSESSING EFFECTIVENESS

Introduction

Evaluating the effectiveness of community policing (CP) poses significant challenges due to its diverse interpretations and implementation methods. Key issues include defining the "community," measuring success beyond traditional crime rates, and ensuring institutional buy-in from all stakeholders. Assessing the effectiveness of community policing moves beyond traditional metrics like arrest numbers to incorporate broader measures of public safety and satisfaction. Evaluation often involves metrics like public satisfaction with police services, citizen perceptions of safety, and willingness to cooperate with law enforcement. Problem-Oriented Policing (POP), a related strategy, uses the SARA model (Scanning, Analysis, Response, and Assessment) to systematically identify and evaluate specific community problems and the effectiveness of tailored solutions. Studies show mixed results. Some evaluations indicate no significant difference in citizen satisfaction or fear of crime over time despite implementation efforts, while others find that strong community engagement can lead to reductions in crime rates and enhanced public trust. Implementation faces numerous practical, organizational, and systemic challenges: difficulty in clearly delineating the "community" and in ensuring that all diverse segments are represented and can effectively partner with police. Police organizational culture can be resistant to change, with officers sometimes reluctant to adopt the decentralized, collaborative approach required by community policing.

Pré-existing mistrust between the police and certain communities, often exacerbated by high-profile use-of-force cases, can hinder effective partnerships and information sharing. Insufficient funding, inadequate training, and staffing shortages limit the ability of departments to fully implement CP initiatives. A lack of standardized, clear benchmarks and indicators for measuring the holistic impact of CP makes it difficult to ascertain "what works and what does not". Future efforts will focus on leveraging technology, enhancing training, and refining evaluation methods. Advanced technologies like AI, data analytics, and drone surveillance will help identify crime patterns and manage resources, but they will require careful implementation to address ethical and privacy concerns. A greater emphasis on EBP, which involves rigorous research and data to inform policing strategies and evaluate their effectiveness, is a key future direction. Increased demand for transparency, accountability, and ethical policing practices will require improved reporting systems and civilian oversight, both of which are crucial for rebuilding public trust. Future officers will need training in areas like de-escalation, cultural competency, and digital skills to effectively engage with diverse communities and address complex, evolving crimes. While specific "Part III" thinkers are not universally indexed, the concepts are largely driven by researchers and organizations such as the Police Executive Research Forum (PERF), the COPS Office (Office of Community Oriented Policing Services) in the US Department of Justice, and academic researchers whose work is often published in journals and government reports (e.g., through the National Institutes of Health or ResearchGate). There is a critical evaluation of community policing programs, analyzing successes and failures in reducing crime and improving community relations.

Key Successes in Community Policing:

Community policing (CP) has yielded several documented successes, primarily in improving the relationship between law enforcement agencies and the communities they serve. A critical evaluation reveals that the impact on crime reduction is often nuanced and tied to specific implementation strategies.

- Improved Community Relations and Trust: CP initiatives consistently show success in increasing public satisfaction, enhancing community trust, and fostering a positive perception of police officers. Programs that facilitate direct, non-enforcement interactions—such as community meetings, youth programs, and coffee-with-a-cop events—bridge divides and encourage cooperation [1].

- Enhanced Information Flow: Stronger relationships encourage residents to share information and report crimes, which improves the flow of actionable intelligence to police departments, often leading to more effective investigations and arrests [1].
- Problem Identification and Resolution: The core principle of CP is the focus on addressing the underlying causes of crime (problem-solving policing). Successful programs utilize community input to identify specific local issues (e.g., specific "hot spots," neglected public spaces, or nuisance properties) and develop tailored solutions beyond traditional enforcement, such as coordinating with municipal services or local non-profits [1].
- Increased Officer Job Satisfaction: When officers feel connected to their beats and see tangible results from their problem-solving efforts, it can lead to improved morale, job satisfaction, and a sense of purpose beyond simply responding to emergency service calls [1].

However, failures and challenges often arise when programs are implemented as temporary measures ("tokenistic policing") rather than as a fundamental organizational philosophy. Common pitfalls include insufficient funding, inadequate training for officers in communication and problem-solving skills, and internal resistance from command staff or police unions who view CP as "soft on crime" or inefficient [1].

Community policing (CP) programs have demonstrated significant success in cultivating trust and fostering positive interactions between police officers and residents. Evaluations of various initiatives highlight that non-enforcement interactions are particularly effective at improving public attitudes toward law enforcement, especially among minority populations where historical tensions may exist.

Specific mechanisms that have proven effective include:

- Brief Door-to-Door Visits: Short, informal visits by officers to residents' homes—not in response to a call for service or an investigation—help personalize the police force, break down perceived barriers, and allow officers and residents to engage as neighbors.
- Community Forums and Meetings: Regular, structured meetings where residents can voice concerns directly to local beat officers and command staff create transparency and a sense of shared responsibility for public safety.
- Targeted Outreach Programs: Initiatives focusing on specific populations, such as youth engagement programs, police athletic leagues, or cultural liaison roles, address specific needs and build long-term rapport.

These positive interactions help shift the relationship from one based purely on authority and enforcement to one grounded in service, mutual respect, and collaborative problem-solving. A comprehensive analysis of studies on community policing often shows that gains in community relations are more robust and consistent than immediate, measurable reductions in crime rates.

Community policing (CP) initiatives frequently succeed in reducing the public's fear of crime, a key metric of program effectiveness, even though the direct impact on crime rates varies across studies and locations. The perceived safety of a neighborhood is as crucial to community well-being as the objective crime statistics.

This reduction in fear is primarily achieved through:

- Increased and Consistent Police Presence: When residents regularly see the same officers patrolling their beat (on foot, bicycle, or in a vehicle), it builds familiarity and provides a tangible sense of security and oversight.
- Enhanced Social Cohesion: By encouraging residents to interact with one another and with law enforcement, CP helps strengthen neighborhood ties. Stronger community bonds lead residents to look out for one another, thereby

reducing feelings of vulnerability and isolation that fuel crime fears.

- Proactive Problem Solving: Addressing visible signs of disorder or neglect (e.g., graffiti, broken streetlights, loitering) through collaborative efforts between police and municipal services signals that the neighborhood is cared for and maintained, which acts as a deterrent to fear (often linked to the "Broken Windows" theory).
- Improved Information and Transparency: Direct communication through community meetings and outreach reduces the spread of rumours and ensures residents have accurate, timely information about local safety issues, allowing them to make informed decisions about their safety rather than relying on generalized anxieties.

These findings highlight that successful community policing is not solely about arrests and response times; it is fundamentally about enhancing the quality of life and perception of safety within a community.

Core Philosophy

Community policing is a core philosophy that emphasizes enhanced information sharing and collaboration to improve public safety. By building trust and robust partnerships with community members and local stakeholders, law enforcement agencies gain access to better local intelligence. This collaboration helps identify and address the underlying causes of crime.

The collaboration is beneficial in several ways:

- Customized Solutions: Working with community members, schools, businesses, and other stakeholders allows the police to gain a more comprehensive understanding of local public safety issues. This leads to the development of tailored, effective solutions that address the specific needs of a neighborhood.
- Proactive Problem-Solving: Partnerships help shift policing from a reactive model to a proactive one. Instead of just

responding to calls for service, police and residents can work together to identify and resolve recurring problems that contribute to crime and disorder.

- Shared Responsibility: This collaborative approach fosters a sense of shared accountability for public safety, helping to bridge the "us versus them" mentality that can exist between the community and the police. When residents feel comfortable communicating with law enforcement, they are more likely to report crimes and share information, which can lead to better outcomes.

Community policing (CP) strategies are highly effective when they utilize a focused, problem-oriented approach tailored to specific, localized issues. This method shifts the focus from simply responding to incidents to proactively addressing the underlying conditions that lead to crime.

The problem-solving component, a core element of CP, helps police and communities address the root causes of disorder through a structured methodology, often referred to as the SARA model (Scanning, Analysis, Response, and Assessment):

- Scanning: Identifying recurring problems through community input and data analysis.
- Analysis: Deeply understanding the causes, scope, and impact of the problem.
- Response: Developing tailored interventions with community partners.
- Assessment: Evaluating the effectiveness of the response and making adjustments.

When implemented correctly, this approach leads to sustainable crime reduction and improved quality of life. Resources and guides on effective problem-oriented policing can be found through organizations such as the Center for Problem-Oriented Policing, which offers numerous guides and case studies on successful implementation.

Failures and Challenges

Research indicates that general CP strategies, such as neighborhood watch programs or storefront offices, do not always lead to a significant actual reduction in crime rates. Effectiveness in crime reduction is strongly linked to targeted, specific problem-solving approaches, rather than a broad, unfocused application of the philosophy.

The success of CP heavily depends on proper execution. Many programs falter due to poor implementation strategies, inadequate officer training, and a lack of clear policy objectives. Challenges also include cultural resistance within traditional police departments, which may view non-enforcement duties as "social work" rather than "real police work". In communities with deeply rooted historical mistrust of law enforcement, achieving meaningful community participation can be difficult. If the community does not trust the police, they are less likely to participate in meetings or share information, undermining a core tenet of CP. Limited resources, including inadequate funding and staffing, often hinder the full implementation of CP programs. This can lead to the practice of "piggybacking" new CP initiatives onto existing methods, which waters down their effectiveness.

Difficulty in High-Crime Areas: Some research suggests that CP may work well in low-crime communities but struggles to be effective in high-crime, resource-deprived areas where socio-economic disparities are significant barriers. In conclusion, community policing's greatest strength lies in its ability to build trust and collaboration between the police and the public. While its ability to single-handedly lower crime rates is debatable without specific, problem-oriented applications, improved community relations are a crucial component for long-term public safety and a more effective criminal justice system.

A critical assessment of community policing (CP) effectiveness reveals it is not a singular solution to all public safety challenges but rather a valuable, nuanced strategy that often achieves its primary goals, though results can vary based on implementation.

Key Findings on Effectiveness

- **Mixed Crime Reduction Results:** The impact of CP on objective crime rates varies and is highly dependent on the specific program, location, and strategies employed. Some initiatives show significant reductions in specific types of crime through problem-oriented approaches, while others show minimal statistical impact on overall crime levels.
- **Significant Success in Community Relations and Trust:** CP consistently excels at improving the relationship between law enforcement and the public. Non-enforcement interactions—such as door-to-door visits, community meetings, and youth outreach programs—effectively build trust and foster positive perceptions of the police, especially within minority populations. A major success area for CP is reducing the public's fear of crime. An increased and consistent police presence in a neighborhood helps residents feel safer and more secure, thereby significantly enhancing their quality of life.
- **Enhanced Information:** By establishing robust partnerships with community members and local stakeholders, police gain better local intelligence and a comprehensive understanding of public safety issues, allowing for tailored, effective solutions.
- **Success of Problem-Oriented Approach:** When strategies are focused and tailored to specific, localized problems (e.g., addressing underlying conditions that lead to crime), CP is highly effective. The problem-solving component helps police and communities address root causes of disorder rather than merely responding to incidents.

In conclusion, community policing programs are successful when implemented as a fundamental organizational philosophy focused on collaboration and problem-solving, rather than as isolated programs. The greatest successes lie in improving community well-being, building trust, and collaboratively addressing the root causes of disorder and fear.

Chapter 9 | THE ROLE OF TECHNOLOGY AND MODERN POLICING

Introduction

Technology has become integral to modern policing, revolutionizing practices by enhancing efficiency, improving public safety, and increasing transparency. Key technologies include data-driven tools such as predictive analytics and GIS, advanced surveillance systems such as CCTV and drones, and investigative aids such as digital forensics and DNA analysis. These advancements streamline administrative tasks, enable faster response times, help prevent crime, and enhance accountability through tools like body-worn cameras. Predictive analytics and GIS help forecast crime hotspots, optimize patrol routes, and allocate resources more effectively. Digital record-keeping and automated systems reduce paperwork and make data easier to store and retrieve. Digital radios, mobile apps, and secure messaging platforms enable faster, more effective communication among officers and with the public.

Improving Public Safety and Crime Prevention

CCTV cameras, drones, and gunshot detection systems provide real-time monitoring and quicker response to incidents. AI and machine learning can help forecast potential threats and allocate resources proactively to prevent crime before it occurs. Digital forensics, facial recognition, and DNA analysis offer powerful tools for identifying suspects and solving cases more efficiently.

Increasing Transparency and Accountability

The devices mentioned earlier record officer interactions, providing an objective record that can improve behavior and provide evidence. The move to digital records and online portals makes police actions more transparent and easier for the public to access and verify. Social media and mobile apps create direct channels for communication, allowing citizens to report crimes and stay informed.

Integration with Community Policing Principles

Social media, data analytics, and body cameras integrate with community policing principles primarily by enhancing communication, transparency, and efficiency, but they also raise significant privacy, data bias, and surveillance concerns.

Technol ogy	Integration (Benefits)	Conflict (Challenges)
SocialMe dia	Community outreach, information sharing, and dialogue. Police can issue timely alerts (road closures, missing persons, crime tips), correct misinformation, humanize officers, and gather intelligence directly from citizens, thereby building trust and collaboration.	Misinformation spread, privacy breaches, and image backlashes from poorly managed communications (e.g., controversial posts or public access to sensitive information). It also creates "digital divides," as some community members (e.g., in rural areas or older demographics) may not use these platforms, potentially excluding them from community engagement efforts.
Data Analytics	Proactive crime prevention, efficient resource allocation, and evidence-based decision-making. By analyzing historical and real-time data from various sources, police can identify crime hotspots and anticipate criminal activity, allowing for targeted patrols and interventions to better protect communities.	Algorithmic bias and fairness concerns, as predictive models trained on historically biased data can lead to the disproportionate over-policing of marginalized communities. Concerns about data security, privacy erosion, and a lack of transparency in how algorithms make decisions can also undermine public trust.
Body Cameras	Increased transparency and accountability in police-citizen interactions, offering an objective record of events that can protect both officers from false accusations and citizens	Privacy concerns for both officers and citizens (especially victims and witnesses) during sensitive encounters. Widespread use also raises complex policy issues regarding data storage, which can access the footage, and potential misuse of

	from misconduct. Footage also serves as valuable evidence and a useful tool for officer training and performance review, which can lead to improved communication and de-escalation tactics.	recordings by law enforcement or the media. Their effectiveness at consistently reducing use of force is mixed, with outcomes heavily dependent on strict activation policies.

Table 9.1

The effective use of modern policing technology requires a delicate balance. When implemented with clear policies, robust oversight, and genuine community engagement, these tools can reinforce community policing principles of transparency and collaboration. Without these safeguards, they risk exacerbating existing societal inequalities and eroding the public trust that community policing strives to build.

In conclusion, technology has become an **indispensable force multiplier** in modern policing, dramatically enhancing operational efficiency, officer safety, and investigative capabilities. Tools like AI-driven predictive analytics, extensive surveillance systems (CCTV, drones, body cameras), and advanced forensics (DNA, biometrics, digital evidence) enable law enforcement to prevent crime more proactively, solve cases faster, and manage data more effectively than ever before.

However, this technological revolution presents significant challenges and ethical considerations. Key issues include: The widespread use of surveillance and data collection technologies raises substantial concerns about mass surveillance and the potential infringement of civil liberties. AI and data analytics tools can perpetuate existing societal and historical biases present in their training data, potentially leading to discriminatory outcomes and the disproportionate policing of minority communities. The high cost of acquiring, implementing, and constantly updating advanced technology, along with the need for specialized officer training, can be a barrier for many departments. For technology to be effective, it must be implemented within a framework of transparency, robust legal oversight, and community engagement to build and maintain public trust. Ultimately, the future of policing lies in a balanced, responsible approach: leveraging innovation to build safer, more efficient communities while simultaneously establishing strong ethical guidelines, legal frameworks, and human oversight to ensure technology is used judiciously and equitably. Continuous dialogue among law enforcement, policymakers, and the public is essential to successfully navigate this complex terrain.

Social Media

Social media, data analytics, and body cameras can be integrated into community policing to enhance transparency, communication, and resource allocation. Still, they raise privacy concerns, the potential for a "tech over human" approach, and the risk of reinforcing existing biases if not implemented thoughtfully.

Integration with Community Policing	Conflict with Community Policing
Enhance outreach and communication to allow police to provide real-time updates on emergencies, missing persons, and road closures.	Risk of misinformation and rumors, which can be amplified quickly and cause public harm or disrupt investigations.
Facilitates citizen engagement and feedback, offering new, accessible channels for community members to report crime tips and voice concerns.	"Dialogic communication" is limited; social media is often used as one-way information broadcast tool rather than a true dialogue platform for collaborative problem-solving.
Builds trust by humanizing officers and showcasing positive police work and initiatives, which can improve public perception.	Potential to reinforce public distrust if the platform is perceived as a mere public relations tool or if media coverage of the footage is sensationalised.

Table 9.2

Data Analytics

Integration with Community Policing	Conflict with Community Policing
Informs resource allocation and targeted intervention strategies, helping police identify crime hotspots and address specific issues proactively.	Risk of bias and "runaway feedback loops" in predictive policing models if historical data is inherently biased, leading to disproportionate policing of marginalized communities.
Aids in problem-solving by identifying patterns and trends in community data (e.g., hospital admissions for knife injuries matched with anti-social behavior reports), allowing for multi-agency responses.	Privacy and ethical concerns over the collection and use of "bigdata," especially sensitive in formation like public health data, without adequate safeguards and transparent community input.
Evaluates the effectiveness of police tactics and interventions by providing evidence-based insights into what works and what doesn't.	Devaluation of professional judgment and community input, as data-driven approaches might prioritize metrics over officers' on-the-ground experience or citizen narratives.

Table 9.3

Body Cameras

Integration with Community Policing	Conflict with Community Policing
Enhances accountability and transparency, providing an objective record of encounters that can protect both citizens and officers from false accusations.	Can create an "illusion of objectivity", as camera footage only captures a limited perspective and can be subject to interpretation or selective use in court and by the media.
Improves officer professionalism and adherence to departmental policies when they know they are being recorded.	Raises significant privacy concerns for both citizens (e.g., during domestic violence calls) and officers (e.g., during private conversations or breaks).

Provides valuable evidence for investigations and court proceedings, leading to more efficient resolution of complaints.	Effectiveness is inconsistent and highly dependent on strict, mandatory activation policies; discretionary use often yields no significant changes in use-of-force incidents or complaints.

Table 9.4

In essence, these technologies can be powerful allies for community policing if their implementation is guided by core principles of **procedural justice, transparency, and community collaboration.** Without a simultaneous commitment to inclusionary policing practices and a focus on building trust, technology alone will fail to address underlying issues in police-community relations.
Technology has become a vital component of modern policing, offering powerful tools for crime prevention, response, and investigation. However, its use is accompanied by significant ethical and organizational challenges that require careful management to balance efficiency with civil liberties and public trust.

Comments and Criticisms

The primary criticism of technology in policing revolves around the balance between public safety and individual rights.

- **Privacy and Surveillance Concerns:** Advanced surveillance technologies, such as facial recognition software (FRT), drones, and automated license plate readers (ALPRs), enable mass surveillance of public spaces, raising substantial privacy concerns for law-abiding citizens. The potential for creating a comprehensive surveillance state is a significant worry for civil liberties advocates.
- **Algorithmic Bias:** Predictive policing software, which uses historical data to forecast crime hotspots, has been widely criticized for potentially reinforcing and amplifying existing racial and socio-economic biases present in historical crime data. This can lead to the over-policing of minority communities and a cycle of discrimination.

- **Misuse and Lack of Oversight:** There are legitimate concerns about the potential for misuse or abuse of technology by individual officers or departments, given the lack of clear policies and robust oversight mechanisms. A lack of transparent legal frameworks for data collection, retention, and access exacerbates these fears.
- **Organizational and Budgetary Challenges:** Outdated infrastructure, interoperability issues across systems, significant implementation and maintenance costs, and internal resistance from officers can hinder effective technology adoption.
- **Over-reliance on Technology:** An over-emphasis on technology may detract from traditional policing methods like community engagement and human intelligence, which remain crucial for building trust and solving complex social problems.

Conclusion

Technology in policing offers undeniable benefits, acting as a force multiplier that enhances efficiency, officer safety, and crime-solving capabilities. Tools like body-worn cameras can improve accountability, while data analytics can help police allocate resources more effectively.

The key conclusion is that technology is a powerful tool, not a replacement for sound policing judgment and community relations. Its successful integration depends entirely on a strong foundation of ethical guidelines, transparency, and public accountability. Without this, technological advancements risk eroding the very public trust essential for effective law enforcement.

Future Direction

The future of policing technology will be defined by further integration of advanced tools and a necessary focus on navigating their ethical implications:

- **Artificial Intelligence and Machine Learning:** AI is set to play an even larger role, from AI-powered dispatch systems and digital assistants for administrative tasks to more sophisticated predictive analytics and forensic analysis.
- **Enhanced Surveillance Tools:** Continued advancements in drones, robotics, and augmented reality (AR) systems will provide officers with real-time situational awareness and remote capabilities.
- **Data Integration and Sharing:** Future efforts will focus on breaking down data silos across agencies to create a unified data platform, enabling better interagency collaboration on complex, transnational crimes.
- **Prioritizing Ethics and Regulation:** As technology becomes more sophisticated, there will be an increased demand for rigorous, independent testing of policing technology for bias and effectiveness, along with clear legal and ethical guardrails developed through collaboration among law enforcement, policymakers, and civil rights advocates.
- **Community Engagement in the Digital Age:** The future direction involves leveraging technology to foster positive community engagement, such as through citizen reporting apps and online forums, to bridge the gap between the police and the public.

Chapter 10 | CONTEMPORARY ISSUES AND FUTURE THINKERS

Chapter 10 on contemporary issues and future thinkers in Critical Race Theory (CRT) focuses on ongoing debates over systemic racism, the concept of legitimacy in law and society, the influence of social justice movements such as Black Lives Matter, and the future evolution and application of the philosophy across various fields.

- **Systemic Racism vs Individual Bias:** A central debate is between the CRT tenet that racism is embedded in laws and institutions (systemic racism) and the view that racism is a matter of individual prejudice.
- **Critiques of Liberalism and Neutrality:** CRT scholars continue to challenge liberal principles such as legal neutrality and colorblindness, arguing that formally colorblind laws often perpetuate racial inequalities in practice.

A major ongoing issue is the intense political controversy surrounding the theory, particularly attempts by conservative lawmakers to ban or restrict the teaching of topics related to systemic racism, equality, and social justice in schools. There is a significant gap between the academic framework of CRT used in legal studies and its often-misrepresented portrayal in public discourse, where any discussion of race or inequality may be labeled as "CRT".

Academic critics sometimes argue that CRT's use of storytelling and personal narratives is unscientific, while proponents contend that these "voices of color" provide essential insights into lived racial experiences that traditional data cannot capture.

Social Justice Movements

Social justice movements like BLM and Land Back movements are informed by CRT's analysis of structural racism and state violence (e.g., police brutality, disproportionate incarceration). CRT provides the analytical framework for understanding the systemic issues these movements address.

Future Thinkers and Evolution of the Philosophy

A key concept for the future is intersectionality, a framework developed by Kimberlé Crenshaw that examines how race intersects with other identities, such as gender, class, and disability, to create unique forms of oppression. CRT has expanded beyond law into numerous fields, including education (DisCrit, TribalCrit), sociology, and women's and gender studies. Future directions include applying CRT methodologies to understand race and inequality beyond the United States, while acknowledging diverse historical and social contexts. Future scholarship advocates radical changes to dismantle systemic inequities across institutions, moving beyond incremental reforms. The chapter emphasizes that CRT remains a dynamic and vital framework for analyzing how race and power interact within society, with ongoing scholarly work aimed at achieving greater racial equity and justice.

Contemporary Issues

Contemporary community policing thinkers are focused on addressing modern challenges such as technological integration, bias, and a shifting understanding of public safety. Building on the foundational work of figures such as Robert Trojanowicz, David H. Bayley, and Mark Moore, the next generation of thought leaders is exploring "knowledge-based" and "data-driven" policing models.

- **Integration of Technology:** A key challenge is effectively using advanced tools like AI, facial recognition, and body cameras while ensuring transparency and protecting civil liberties. The potential for algorithmic bias in predictive policing tools is a major point of concern and research.

Incidents of police misconduct and social unrest have highlighted the critical need to rebuild public trust, particularly in

minority communities. This requires genuine transparency, accountability mechanisms, and fair procedures.
Police are increasingly the first responders to a wide range of social issues (e.g., mental health crises, homelessness), which often consume significant resources. New thinking involves co-responder models that pair officers with social workers to address these underlying problems more humanely and effectively. The rise of online fraud and sophisticated cybercrime necessitates new digital skills for officers and enhanced collaboration between local, national, and international agencies. Recruitment and retention of qualified personnel, along with the need for ongoing training in digital competencies, de-escalation, and community interaction, are persistent organizational challenges.

Future Thinkers and Direction

Future thinkers are generally focused on evolving the community policing philosophy to be more adaptable, evidence-based, and integrated with broader community services.

- **David Weisburd & Anthony Braga:** These academics are prominent advocates for evidence-based policing and "hot spots" policing, which uses rigorous analysis to focus police resources on specific geographic areas or problems where crime is concentrated. Their work emphasizes data-driven decision-making.
- **Tyler, Tom R.:** Known for his work on procedural justice, Tyler's research highlights the importance of fair and respectful treatment in police interactions as a key driver of police legitimacy and public cooperation. His thinking continues to shape approaches to building trust.
- **Jeremy M. Wilson & Graeme Blair:** Their recent work and experiments in various countries have focused on rigorously evaluating the effectiveness of community policing, exploring whether it consistently builds citizen trust or reduces crime in different contexts. They advocate for an evidence-based approach to policy decisions.

- **Abid Jan:** As a contemporary thought leader, Jan emphasizes a collaborative, risk-driven, and prevention-oriented policing model. He argues for integrating risk-prevention and targeted social development into core policing strategies to reduce calls for emergency services.
- **Riane Eisler:** Through her Cultural Transformation Theory, Eisler has provided a framework for a "New Community Policing" based on a partnership model of social organization. This approach emphasizes collaboration, shared responsibility, and cultural relevance in police-community relationships.

The future of community policing lies in a "knowledge-based" approach that responsibly uses data and technology, focuses on prevention and restorative justice, and integrates law enforcement efforts with a wide range of community and social services to address underlying problems.

Conclusion

The evolution of policing, from traditional to community- and data-driven models, highlights a core challenge: how to effectively ensure public safety and maintain order in an increasingly complex and digitalized world while simultaneously building and maintaining public trust and legitimacy. The prevailing conclusion among contemporary thinkers is that no single policing model is sufficient. Instead, a hybrid approach is necessary, integrating effective elements of various models (traditional, community, problem-oriented, intelligence-led) tailored to the specific needs and expectations of diverse communities. The ultimate success of any strategy hinges not just on new technology or tactics, but on a foundation of ethical conduct, transparency, and accountability.

Critics

Critics point to several ongoing issues with contemporary policing efforts and the ideas of future thinkers:

- **Uneven Effectiveness:** Community policing is criticized for working well in low-crime, stable communities but often failing to build trust or reduce crime effectively in high-crime, disadvantaged areas that need it most.
- **Technological Bias:** The use of predictive analytics and surveillance technology is a major criticism, as these tools can entrench and amplify existing racial and social biases present in historical data, leading to the over-policing of minority groups.
- **Organizational Inertia:** Significant cultural and organizational barriers within police departments, such as resistance to change, command-and-control structures, and outdated performance metrics (e.g., valuing arrests over problem-solving outcomes), impede the adoption of new, more effective strategies.
- **Mission Creep:** Police forces are increasingly diverted to handle complex social problems like mental health crises, homelessness, and substance abuse, for which they are not adequately trained or equipped. Critics argue that this dilutes their core mission and consumes resources, leading to lower detection rates for crimes such as online fraud.
- **Accountability Deficit:** A lack of robust, independent oversight and accountability mechanisms for police misconduct continues to erode public confidence and legal cynicism, a cultural belief that the legal system is unfair and unresponsive.

Future Outlook and Way Forward

The way forward, as envisioned by contemporary thinkers like David Weisburd, Anthony Braga, and Tom Tyler, involves a networked, knowledge-based, and community-defined approach to policing.

- **Evidence-Based and Data-Driven Policing:** The future lies in rigorous evaluation of policing tactics to determine what works, where, and why. This involves using data responsibly to focus resources on specific problem areas (hot spot policing) while ensuring fairness and transparency.

- **Integrated Responses to Social Issues:** The development of co-responder models (pairing officers with social workers or mental health professionals) will become standard practice to address the complex social demands placed on police, thereby reducing the burden on law enforcement and improving outcomes for vulnerable individuals.
- **Agile and Networked Organizations:** Police agencies must move away from rigid, hierarchical command structures toward more flexible, networked models that empower individual officers to make informed, on-the-spot decisions aligned with organizational values and community needs.
- **Leveraging Technology with Guardrails:** Future policing will be highly tech-enabled, utilizing AI and enhanced data sharing, but must be accompanied by strong ethical guidelines, legal frameworks, and public input to prevent misuse and protect civil liberties.
- **National Standards with Local Application:** There is a growing call for national standards in training, recruitment, and use-of-force policies to ensure consistency and professionalism across diverse departments. These standards, however, must be flexible enough to be tailored to the unique needs and priorities defined by the local communities themselves.
- **Recruitment and Training Reform:** A significant focus must be placed on improving recruitment to reflect the communities served and enhancing training in de-escalation, cultural awareness, and interpersonal skills, not just tactical abilities.

The pathway to the future requires a holistic transformation of police culture, leadership, and community partnership, utilizing the current challenges as a "burning platform" for fundamental, lasting change.

Chapter 11 | CONCLUSION: SUMMARIZESTHE ENDURING LEGACY AND FUTURE POTENTIAL OF COMMUNITY POLICING THOUGHT

This chapter summarizes the enduring legacy and future potential of community policing thought. Key thinkers and developers of community policing theory and practice include Sir Robert Peel, James Q. Wilson, and George Kelling.

- **Sir Robert Peel (19th Century):** Known as the "father of modern policing," Peel established the principles of democratic policing in 1829, which emphasized that police needed the public's consent, trust, and cooperation to be effective. This is considered the earliest form of the community policing paradigm.
- **James Q. Wilson and George L. Kelling:** These criminologists introduced the influential "Broken Windows" theory in a 1982 Atlantic Monthly article. This theory posits that visible signs of physical and social disorder (like a single unrepaired broken window) can create an environment that encourages further, more serious crime and social decay. Their work argued for police methods that addressed minor crimes and disorder to maintain an atmosphere of order and lawfulness, thus preventing more serious offenses.
- **George Kelling (and William Bratton):** Kelling later worked as a consultant in New York City, where William Bratton, as Police Commissioner, implemented policies based on the "Broken Windows" theory in the 1990s, focusing on "quality of life" offenses such as fare evasion and graffiti.

- **Robert Trojanowicz and Bonnie Bucqueroux:** The Founders of the National Center for Community Policing at Michigan State University, they authored works such as *Community Policing: A Contemporary Perspective* and *Community Policing: How to Get Started*, which provided frameworks for implementing community policing.
- **David H. Bayley:** A prominent scholar who has written extensively on policing, including the challenges and potential pitfalls of implementing community policing.
- **Wesley Skogan:** Known for his extensive research on community policing and neighborhood dynamics, including studies in Chicago on the impact of encounters with police and the relationship between disorder and crime.
- **Herman Goldstein:** Developed the concept of Problem-Oriented Policing (POP), which involves a systematic process (often using the SARA model: Scanning, Analysis, Response, and Assessment) to examine and address underlying community problems that give rise to crime and disorder. This concept is a core component of modern community policing strategies.
- **Elinor Ostrom:** A Nobel laureate economist whose work in public management included studies on policing and the concept of coproduction, emphasizing the role of citizens in producing public safety.

Enduring Legacy

The enduring legacy of community policing lies in its fundamental shift from a reactive, isolated enforcement model to a proactive, collaborative philosophy that views the public as an essential co-producer of safety and security. Its future potential is centered on integrating advanced technology with community engagement to address increasingly complex, transnational, and digital crime landscapes.

The legacy of community policing is rooted in several core principles that have permanently influenced modern policing thought and practice:

- **Building Trust and Legitimacy:** Community policing emphasizes building strong, positive relationships and trust between law enforcement and the communities they serve, a crucial element for police legitimacy and public cooperation.
- **Problem-Solving Focus:** It moved beyond simply responding to incidents by promoting proactive, problem-oriented policing (POP) strategies, such as the SARA model (Scanning, Analysis, Response, and Assessment), to address the underlying causes of crime and disorder.
- **Shared Responsibility:** The philosophy established that police are the public and the public are the police, fostering shared accountability for public safety and leveraging community resources for crime prevention.
- **Improved Public Perception and Satisfaction:** Studies have shown that community policing strategies significantly increase citizen satisfaction and improve perceptions of police conduct and accessibility.

FuturePotential

The future of community policing involves adapting these core principles to new challenges and opportunities, particularly through:

- **Technological Integration:** Future policing will leverage data analytics, artificial intelligence, and real-time crime centers to inform strategies and identify crime hotspots. This data-driven approach, sometimes called "intelligence-driven community policing," will require officers to develop new digital competencies.
- **Enhanced Community Engagement:** The core need for community relationships remains paramount, with future engagement expanding into digital spaces through social

media and virtual platforms to maintain open communication channels and foster ongoing dialogue.

- **Specialized and Preventive Approaches:** There is a growing shift towards preventive and restorative justice approaches, where some social issues and conflict resolution may be handled by a wider range of community professionals, such as social workers, in partnership with the police.
- **Addressing Transnational and Cybercrime:** As the criminal landscape becomes more sophisticated and transnational, community policing thought will need to evolve to address these complex threats, requiring greater collaboration among local, state, federal, and international agencies.

Ultimately, the thought leader concludes that community policing has established an enduring framework for collaborative public safety, and its future success hinges on integrating technology and adapting engagement strategies to an evolving, digital, and diverse society while remaining anchored in community partnerships. Community policing is defined by its fundamental shift in perspective: effective public safety is a shared responsibility between the police and the public. The future potential lies in evolving this philosophy to be more evidence-based, technologically sophisticated, and centered on social equity, while navigating significant managerial and ethical challenges.

Recommendations

To realize the future potential of community policing, several key recommendations emerge from the analysis of past and contemporary thinkers:

- Police agencies should rigorously evaluate their programs and prioritize strategies scientifically proven to reduce crime and build trust, as advocated by thinkers like Anthony Braga and David Weisburd.

- All interactions with the public must be guided by principles of fairness, transparency, and respect, drawing on Tom Tyler's research to enhance police legitimacy and citizen cooperation.
- New technologies like AI and data analytics should be adopted, and clear, transparent policies and oversight mechanisms should be established with public input to prevent bias and protect civil liberties.
- Partnerships with mental health professionals, social workers, and other community services should be developed to better address complex social problems, freeing up police resources for traditional law enforcement tasks.
- Police leadership must champion a culture shift from a reactive, incident-driven model to a proactive, problem-solving, and community-integrated approach, a core challenge identified by Mark Moore.

Critical Comments and Drawbacks

Despite its promise, the implementation of community policing faces significant criticism and inherent drawbacks: The philosophy is often treated as a temporary program rather than a fundamental organizational change, leading to uneven results and a reversion to traditional policing under pressure. Effective community policing requires significant investment in time, training, and resources, which many cash-strapped municipalities struggle to provide consistently. Measuring the true "public value" (e.g., trust, fear reduction, community cohesion) created by community policing is difficult, making it challenging to justify funding compared to easily quantifiable metrics like arrest rates. There is a risk that police can use community engagement to simply manage or control community groups rather than genuinely empowering them to co-produce safety solutions.

Future Direction

The future direction of community policing is a hybrid model that is adaptable and responsive to evolving societal needs:

The future will see policing deeply informed by data analytics and social science research to target the root causes of crime and disorder. There will be a greater emphasis on restorative justice approaches and crime prevention through social development, moving beyond the traditional punitive justice system. Future models will prioritize robust, independent oversight and accountability mechanisms to ensure ethical conduct and build trust, regardless of technological advancements. The future involves genuine partnerships in which communities co-define public safety priorities and work collaboratively with police and other agencies to achieve them, reflecting a true partnership model of social organization.

Conclusion

This chapter summarizes the enduring legacy and future potential of community policing thought. The enduring legacy of community policing thought, originating with pioneers like Robert Trojanowicz, is the unshakeable premise that effective policing is impossible without public trust and cooperation. Its foundational concepts of decentralization, empowerment, and partnership provided a vital critique of traditional, isolated policing models. The future potential of this philosophy lies in its ability to adapt to a rapidly changing world defined by technology, social complexity, and diverse community needs. By embracing evidence-based practices, responsibly leveraging technology, and genuinely sharing authority and responsibility with the communities they serve, police can evolve into legitimate, effective, and respected partners in the pursuit of public safety and a just society.

Bibliography

1. Brayne, S. (2017). *Predict and surveil: Data, discretion, and the future of policing*. Oxford University Press.
2. Chriss, J. J. (2022). *Beyond community policing: From early American beginnings to the 21st century*. Routledge.
3. Dharavath, L. (n.d.). *Bharat mein samudayik policing*.
4. Friedmann, R. R. (1992). *Community policing: Comparative perspectives and prospects*. St. Martin's Press.
5. Goldstein, H. (1990). *Problem-oriented policing*. McGraw-Hill.
6. Greene, J. R., & Mastrofski, S. D. (Eds.). (1988). *Community policing: Rhetoric or reality*. Praeger.
7. Grogan, B. (n.d.). *Guardians of the community: Uniting communities through Sir Robert Peel's time-honored principles*.
8. Harcourt, B. E. (2001). *Illusion of order: The false promise of broken windows policing*. Harvard University Press.
9. Kappeler, V. E., Gaines, L. K., & Schaefer, B. P. (2015). *Community policing: A contemporary perspective*. Routledge.
10. Keay, S., & Kirby, S. (2021). *Improving intelligence analysis in policing*. Routledge.
11. Kelling, G. L., & Coles, C. M. (1996). *Fixing broken windows: Restoring order and reducing crime in our communities*. Free Press.
12. Manning, P. K., & Mastrofski, S. D. (Eds.). (1997). *Trust and confidence in the police*.
13. Miller, L. S., & Hess, K. M. (2008). *Community policing: Theory and practice*. Wadsworth.
14. Nobo, C., & Tyler, T. R. (2023). *Legitimacy-based policing and the promotion of community vitality*.
15. O'Reilly, C. (2024). *Neighbourhood policing: Context, practices and challenges*.
16. Palgrave Macmillan. (n.d.). *Policing and intelligence in the global big data era* (Vol. II).
17. Parsons, D. A., & Kremling, J. (2016). *Community policing today: Issues, controversies, and innovations*. Sage Publications.

18. Peak, K. J. (Ed.). (2013). *Encyclopedia of community policing and problem solving.* Sage Publications.
19. Peak, K. J., & Glensor, R. W. (2012). *Community policing and problem solving: Strategies and practices.* Pearson.
20. Skogan, W. G., & Hartnett, S. M. (1997). *Community policing, Chicago style.* Oxford University Press.
21. Trojanowicz, R., & Bucqueroux, B. (1990). *Community policing: How to get started.* Anderson Publishing.
22. Tyler, T. R. (1990). *Why people obey the law.* Yale University Press.
23. Wickes, R., & Mazerolle, L. (2013). *Crime and disorder in community context.* Cambridge University Press.
24. Wilson, J. Q., & Kelling, G. L. (1982). Broken windows: The police and neighborhood safety. *The Atlantic Monthly.*
25. Wisler, D., & Onwudiwe, I. D. (Eds.). (2009). *Community policing: International patterns and comparative perspectives.* CRC Press.
26. Zimring, F. E. (2011). *The city that became safe: New York's lessons for urban crime and its control.* Oxford University Press.

THE PROMINENT COMMUNITY POLICING THINKERS AND THEIR BOOKS

1. Robert Trojanowicz ("The Father of Community Policing")

- **Book:** *Community Policing: How to Get Started*
    - *Significance:* This is considered a foundational text that provides a roadmap for shifting from traditional to community-oriented policing.

2. Victor E. Kappeler & Larry K. Gaines

- **Book:** *Community Policing: A Contemporary Perspective*
    - *Significance:* Now in its 8th edition, this book is a key text for understanding the evolution of community policing and its practical implementation.

3. Kenneth J. Peak & Ronald W. Glensor

- **Book:** *Community Policing and Problem Solving: Strategies and Practices*
    - *Significance:* Focuses heavily on the practical application of problem-oriented policing to reduce crime and disorder.
- **Book:** *Encyclopedia of Community Policing and Problem Solving* (Edited by Kenneth J. Peak)

4. Linda Miller & Karen M. Hess

- **Book:** *Community Policing: Partnerships for Problem Solving*

- *Significance:* Covers the history, philosophy, and practical, day-to-day strategies for building community partnerships.

5. Other Key Thinkers and Academic Texts

- **Arvind Verma & Dilip K. Das:** *Police Leaders as Thinkers*
- **Michael Palmiotto:** *Community Policing: A Policing Strategy for the 21st Century*
- **Dennis P. Rosenbaum:** *The Challenge of Community Policing: Testing the Promises*
- **Dominique Wisler & Ihekwoaba D. Onwudiwe:** *Community Policing: International Patterns and Comparative Perspectives*
- **Mike Brogden & Preeti Nijhar:** *Community Policing*

THEORIES OF COMMUNITY POLICING

1. **Broken Windows Theory (Kelling & Wilson):** Suggests that visible signs of disorder (e.g., graffiti, vandalism) create an environment that encourages serious crime. Addressing minor issues strengthens community safety.
2. **Social Disorganization Theory:** Posits that crime stems from weak social bonds and instability in neighborhoods, which community policing aims to fix by strengthening community cohesion.
3. **Social Capital Theory:** Highlights that building trust and social networks (capital) within a community increases its capacity to prevent crime collectively.
4. **Problem-Oriented Policing (Herman Goldstein):** A precursor and cousin to community policing, which focuses on analyzing specific, recurring problems to develop custom solutions.
5. **Structuration Theory:** Used to understand how police-community interaction (action) can change the formal structures of police organizations.

KEY THINKERS AND INFLUENCERS

1. **Sir Robert Peel:** Considered the father of modern policing, his "Peelian principles" established that the police are the public and the public are the police, focusing on relationship-building.
2. **Herman Goldstein:** Developed the concept of Problem-Oriented Policing (POP), which is crucial for identifying underlying issues in the community.
3. **George Kelling & James Q. Wilson:** Authored the "Broken Windows" article, changing the focus to order maintenance and community partnership.
4. **Robert Trojanowicz:** A major proponent of community policing in the US, emphasizing the need for foot patrol and citizen partnership.
5. **John Alderson:** A British Chief Constable who popularized "communal policing" in the 1970s as a way to decentralize police work.

KEY CONCEPTS IN ACTION

1. **Decentralization:** Moving police services from central headquarters to neighborhoods.
2. **Empowerment:** Giving officers and citizens the authority to solve problems together.
3. **Partnership:** Actively involving residents in patrolling (e.g., Neighborhood Watch) and decision-making.